Kabbalah and Astrology

By the same author:

Adam & The Kabbalistic Trees
A Kabbalistic Universe
The Way of Kabbalah
Introduction to the World of Kabbalah
The Kabbalist at Work
Kabbalah and Exodus
School of the Soul
Psychology and Kabbalah
The Kabbalistic Tree of Life
The Anointed–a *Kabbalistic novel*
Anatomy of Fate
Path of a Kabbalist
A Kabbalistic View of History

By Other Publishers:

Kabbalah—The Divine Plan (HarperCollins)
Kabbalah, Tradition of Hidden Knowledge (Thames & Hudson)
Astrology, The Celestial Mirror (Thames & Hudson)
As Above So Below (Stuart & Watkins)

Kabbalah and Astrology
Z'ev ben Shimon Halevi

Kabbalah
Society

Bet El Trust
Registered Charity No. 288712
This edition published by:

www.kabbalahsociety.org
E-mail: books@kabbalahsociety.org

First published in 2000 by Urania Trust
Revised Edition 2009 by Kabbalah Society
Copyright © Z'ev ben Shimon Halevi 2000, 2009

A CIP catalogue record for this book
is available from the British Library

ISBN: 978-1-909171-03-9

Printed and bound by Lightning Source UK Ltd., Milton Keynes
Design by Tree of Life Publishing
www.treeoflifepublishing.co.uk

For Solomon Ibn Gabirol
Maggid and Friend

Contents

Illustrations

Figure 1—KABBALISTIC ASTROLOGY
Information is one thing but real knowledge is quite another. One may have all the data for a birth chart and yet not perceive its essence. Astrology is an art, not a science. This means that the horoscope is seen as an image that contains the person's being. This comes only from great experience or a metaphysical and symbolic foundation of an esoteric tradition, such as Kabbalah. In this picture, an astrologer with spiritual knowledge perceives the principals behind the physical universe. (Woodcut, 16th century.)

Preface

Every life has an individual pattern. Some lives are full of incident and some are quiet, while others seem graced by good fortune or cursed by ill luck. Why is this? And what, many ask, is it that pre-determines the flow of events and precipitates the crises that occur in our path through life? Astrologers often describe in great detail the effects of this or that celestial configuration but rarely define the causes or the mechanism of how these actually influence us. The answers are to be found in the ancient teachings behind astrology which add a spiritual dimension and indicate the Divine purpose of the anatomy of fate.

Figure 2—SYSTEM
Astrology is the result of millennia of study. It is a composite of thousands of celestial observations that seemed to relate to patterns of human behaviour and character. What is shown here are the various systems and symbols that interact. On the edge are the twelve psychological types of the zodiac. Inside this are the mundane Houses, through which those types manifest in the everyday world. Within this circle come the triads of the four elements of temperament and the celestial rulers of each sign in their negative and positive modes. At the centre are the classical gods, metals, ages and sefirot associated with the Solar system. (*Cosmic Clock*, Halevi.)

Introduction

A birth chart is more than the positions and angles of the celestial bodies in the heavens. It is a progress report on the result of karma. This universal law, known in Kabbalah as 'measure for measure', was recognised by Sir Isaac Newton, the 17th century physicist. He showed that no action was without a reaction. This is not just a cosmic rule within the physical world but a real factor in the psychological and spiritual realms. No life, good or bad, is without its consequences. This is set out in the horoscope.

According to many spiritual traditions including Kabbalah, the Jewish esoteric teaching, reincarnation is the norm. An individual soul passes through many lives. In each, the sum of its successes and failures will manifest at the moment of birth to set out the course of the next fate. The horoscope also indicates all the lessons designed to aid and educate that soul's development on the path of self-realisation, if one knows how to discern them.

This book brings together two ancient disciplines, astrology and Kabbalah, in the light of modern psychology so that a greater insight may be achieved when considering the anatomy of fate.

xiv

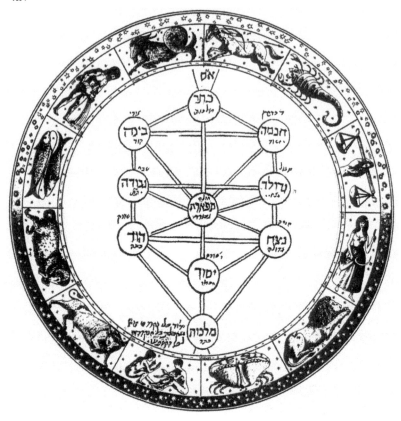

Figure 3—KABBALAH
Although known by this name only since medieval times, the Tradition dates back
to ancient Mesopotamia where the image of a sacred tree was used to symbolise
Existence and its laws. Here within the zodiac is the kabbalistic Tree of Life. It is
a metaphysical version of what had been transmitted in myth, fable and symbol
for centuries. With the advent of philosophy in the Middle Ages, it was decided
to present esoteric ideas in diagrammatic form. This was applied later to astrology,
so as to deepen the understanding of the way fate and destiny worked.
(Cordovero's *Tree of Life*, 16th century.)

1. Knowledge

The first premise to be accepted is that the universe is not a chaos but governed by a set of laws. While everything appears to be in motion and, at times, seems disordered and disjointed, in fact Existence is a very precisely organised entity. If it were not so, then chaos would rule and there would be no process of birth, growth and death, evolution or resolution. An understanding of the regulation and aim of Existence is the purpose of the pursuit of knowledge.

This began when the first human beings on Earth started to examine their environment. Initially they were bound by instinct, that inherent body of experience gained by the mineral, vegetable and animal kingdoms which was passed on in the chemistry, cells and organic intelligence of their bodies. As such, the earliest human reactions to terrestrial conditions were little more than natural reflexes, just like those of their ape cousins. But a human being is more than a highly evolved physical organism. Men and women have a mind that considers more than the immediate environment. It can speculate about the past, present and future and come to conclusions.

This capacity to ponder, experiment and create is unique to humanity. It is not an accident but the result of a Divine plan that also created the atoms, the elements, the stars, the planets and the complex interacting ecology of life on Earth. Humanity might have been born into a fleshly body, or put on a 'coat of skin' as the Bible says, but it is clear that its ability to be reflective and creative is of quite a different order to that of the most advanced of apes.

Because of this unique capacity, mankind has accumulated a body of knowledge over tens of thousands of years. This has been applied to such a degree that humanity has greatly altered the face of the planet. The mastery of fire, air, water and earth led to the agricultural and early technical revolution that was to encroach on the wilderness. This gave rise to permanent villages, towns and urban culture. With cities came specialists who could consider matters beyond basic needs. Building upon the work of tribal shamans, the priesthood added methodical study to a visionary understanding of Existence. Here began two lines of knowledge.

Out of the observation of natural phenomena came the exact plotting of the rhythms of the Sun, Moon and stars. While this data was useful for religious and economic reasons, it initiated an enquiry into the meaning behind the symbols of intuition, inspiration and revelation about the universe that had been handed down. There seemed to be some kind of coincidence between events on Earth and what occurred in the heavens. Besides bad or good harvests, there were periods of peace and war that appeared to be synchronised with certain celestial configurations.

As civilisation developed, a detailed record was kept of the various motions in the sky and their apparent influence on terrestrial events. It was noted, for example, that when the blood-red planet Mars was in particular parts of the sky, conflicts arose not only between individuals but also between city states. Moreover Saturn, a dull and slow-moving 'wanderer', seemed to put a restraining but steadying hand on mundane affairs when it was in certain celestial positions. Indeed, all the visible planets and the two luminaries, Sun and Moon, apparently had effects of varying strength when related to particular sections of the zodiacal belt that encompassed the heavens.

Between the first empires of Mesopotamia and the peak of Roman power, a whole body of information about celestial influences had been gathered. This was co-ordinated into a domelike map of the heavens with a grid system that could plot the exact positions of the celestial bodies. By this time the band of the Zodiac had been resolved into twelve symbols that defined the characteristics of each section. They were not, as many believe, modelled on the twelve constellations which would eventually shift their position and patterns. The symbols were based upon the twelve stages of the seasons and the temperament of people born in the period when the Sun was in each sign. Thus, for example, Leo described in its radiant mane the thirty hot, dry days of high Summer and the Fiery, expansive disposition of people incarnated at this time; while the sign of the Goat defined the cold, dry nadir of Winter and the stolid ambition of a Capricorn's nature as the Sun began to climb after the solstice.

Symbolism was the language of knowledge during this seminal period. While scientific, technological information was vital to plot an astrological situation, it was the mode of art that was used to explain and demonstrate universal and archetypal principles. For example, the

Figure 4—MYSTIC AND PHILOSOPHER
In any genuine esoteric tradition, mysticism and philosophy are one and the same. A question about the universe, the human condition and the origin of all are considered by the heart and head, as well as from a practical view point. Conclusions are reached after much pondering and deep insights during meditation. Unless they square with experience and esoteric knowledge acquired though revelation, they are not taken seriously. Today most science lacks a philosophic base and abhors any mystical dimension. The so-called Age of Reason lost the faculty of imagination. (The Philosophical Mystic, 17th century print.)

twelve basic psychological types were set out in the twelve tribes of
Israel and the twelve disciples of Jesus. These archetypes were sub-
divided into Solar, Lunar, Mercurial, Venusian, Martial, Jovian and
Saturnine personalities which related to the mythical gods. Such
symbolic images were common to ancient humanity which believed
that the heavens and the Earth were ruled by various deities.

The celestial gods were perceived to occupy an invisible zone, also
inhabited by the dead and the unborn. Here the idea of other realities
has to be taken into account, as this is a basic esoteric premise. The
physical universe is but the lowest level of the several realms that
compose Existence. The primitive and ancient cultures accepted this
notion, not as a theological or philosophical concept but as an
experiential fact. This is borne out, for example, by the world-wide
belief in ghosts, spirits, Heaven and Hell.

Astrology was a combination of carefully tabulated observation
and imagination. Unfortunately, by Roman times it had become, at
street level, a superstitious cult. This was also true of many degenerate
esoteric practices, such as reducing the idea of the soul's immortality
to a ritual of mummifying the body. Nevertheless, serious astrologers
continued to practise the art until it was revitalised by the Arabs and
Jews of the early medieval epoch. They enriched it further with their
discoveries so that, by the time that Western European interest was
aroused, it became part of a crucial debate between religion and
philosophy on the issue of free will versus predetermination.

(Philosophy is the way of reason and, during the Middle Ages, it
became the testing and proving tool of religious faith) Astrology came
somewhere between the two 'truths' in that it used both observation
and intuition. While astrology could not be logically explained, it
appeared to work to such a degree that one Pope chose to be crowned
on a day recommended by his astrologer. Indeed, no general would
start a battle and no sea captain set sail without considering the
celestial situation. The Middle Ages and Renaissance were a great
high point for astrology. No monarch, merchant or physician would
make a decision before considering the positions of the Sun, Moon
and planets.

All this came to an abrupt end when Galileo turned his telescope up
into the sky. He and other scientists so undermined accepted ancient
concepts by their experiments and discoveries that the old world
picture of the universe, supported by religious theology, virtually
evaporated in Europe. The rise of pure science and the breakdown of

the medieval order led educated people to discard astrology as a collection of superstitions. Within a generation the subject, once taught in many European universities, was dropped as celestial mechanics became the fashion. Centuries of study about the influence of the heavens upon the Earth were all but forgotten. Astrology was regarded as only of interest to charlatans and eccentrics.

Among the 'eccentrics' was Sir Isaac Newton, sometimes called the last of the magicians and the first of the modern scientists. He was not only well acquainted with astrology but was interested in alchemy and Kabbalah. He belonged to a circle of eminent people that included Sir Christopher Wren, Robert Boyle and Elias Ashmole. They were fascinated by the esoteric teachings that had almost been obliterated by the new epoch of so-called 'Reason' in which the realms of soul, spirit and the Divine were set aside in the pursuit of physics.

Science, as the study of the purely material aspect of reality, advanced with such leaps and bounds from the 17th century on, that by the 19th century it had become, for many, a form of religion that could answer any question, given time. Geology and Darwin's theory of evolution destroyed Biblical chronology and the belief that humanity had descended from Paradise. However, while science seemed to offer an explanation of the origin of the universe, it could not identify its purpose. Providentially, in the 20th century a series of discoveries about the nature of matter and time shook the mechanistic viewpoint and reopened the door to metaphysics and mysticism.

Beyond the atom there appeared to be—nothing. Moreover, energy and matter were continually disappearing and reappearing after the universe had emerged out of nothingness, as a point of light, just as many creation myths described. For this science had no explanation. In addition, radio telescopes and other sensitive instruments revealed that the universe was filled with previously unknown emissions, field forces and interactions. It was discovered that the Sun, Moon and Jupiter indeed had an effect upon the cycles of Nature, the stock market and electronic communications. Even time could no longer be seen as a simple, moving moment. It had other dimensions, such as repetition, retention of the past and precognition of the future.

Such discoveries re-aroused interest in astrology, then part of a revival of the occult and spiritual movement in the 1970s. With the aid of computers, astrology underwent a transformation. The technical evolution was added to by the work of contemporary psychologists whose understanding of mythical archetypes and modern clinical observation keyed into the symbolism of astrology. Out of this emerged a new phase of celestial studies. This examined the dynamic and structure of the psyche, the function of fate and the meaning of destiny. Here is where Kabbalah, then also being re-examined, provided a deeper and wider picture of Existence, humanity's place and its purpose. Esoteric knowledge was reinstated as a relevant study.

2. *Esoterics*

The word esoteric means to be 'hidden'. The implication is not of 'secret' but 'unnoticed', because the more subtle laws and processes of Existence cannot be recognised by those who only perceive the universe through the senses. An individual may be well educated, devout in religion and even a renowned philosopher but yet be totally blind to what an observant peasant might know about Nature spirits or the dead. For example, many people sensitive to atmosphere can tell whether a house is a happy home or otherwise. This is because any long-term routine or dramatic event saturates the fabric of a building with a subtle field force that takes time to discharge, sometimes centuries. This principle is accepted in science in that heat can be contained; but not indefinitely, for it will disperse since an equilibrium of temperature must eventually be restored. The same law applies to the psychological and spiritual domains which are beyond any current scientific instrument's capacity to detect. The study of these occult dimensions is the science of esoterica.

From very early times it was clear that some people, men or women, were more aware of these hidden dimensions. Besides being able to dowse for water, follow energy lines across a landscape or communicate with the 'Ancestors', such individuals could identify the emanations given off by celestial bodies. This was possible because cosmic frequencies resonate with the psyche, which is based upon the same universal model. Structures like Stonehenge and the Pyramids were designed to focus and concentrate incoming celestial influxes, like the giant horns used in wartime to hear distant aircraft. The priests would describe such phenomena in mythological images or as the 'Music of the Spheres'. Modern astronomers call such frequencies the electro-magnetic signature of celestial bodies or astronomical zones. They define them in contemporary scientific terms.

Ancient astronomers were especially interested in the exact effect of these influxes on the Earth. The only difference between them and

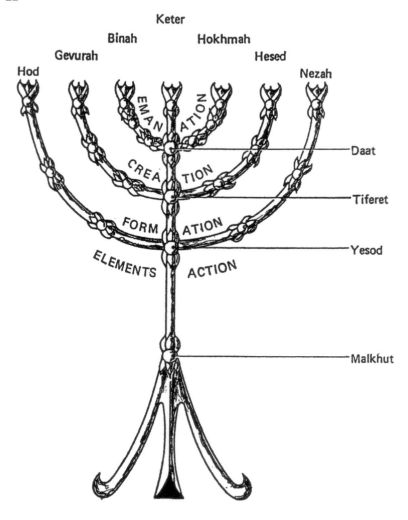

Figure 5—MENORAH
This seven-branched candlestick was to be found in Moses' Tabernacle and
Solomon's Temple. It sets out, in symbolic form, the metaphysics of Existence. It
has right and left wings that signify the active and passive aspects of the Universe
and a central column that represents an axis of balance. This
corresponds to the Chinese Yang, Yin and Tao. There are ten nodal points and
twenty-two decorations. These represent the Ten Numbers, or Divine Attributes,
and the paths that connect them. Between the arms are the spaces that define the
four distinct but interconnected universes. The Menorah was made of pure gold,
indicating unity and Divinity. (Drawing by Halevi.)

their modern counterparts was that they used their minds as telescopic tools. Human consciousness is still the finest instrument on the planet. Einstein, the 20th century cosmologist, was well in line with the tradition of blending observation and intuition when he conceived the Theory of Relativity.

(The classical Greek philosopher and mystic, Plato, recognised that behind whatever existed on Earth there was an archetype. Everything, from a stone to the Moon, was based upon a non-physical form which, in turn, related to an abstract idea. Thus there was the substance of a stone, its flint or granite form, and the idea of stoniness which never changed. Such an archetypal concept was, in its way, more permanent than any rock or mountain. This indicated to Plato that there were three basic universes: of matter, form and ideas. A fourth level was a higher World where these lower realities originated. This is called the Divine realm in Kabbalah.

The actuality of these 'hidden Worlds' was corroborated by mystics of every culture who, in an awakened state of meditation, contemplation or ritual, experienced three distinct upper universes. These levels were defined by various names; but all agreed that the topmost was concerned with the Eternal while the three lower Worlds related to various degrees of actualising the potentiality of Divinity. The bottommost universe was the full manifestation in physicality of all the realms above.

Most early communities believed that when the physical body died, the soul survived and even hovered about its home for a while before it departed into the higher Worlds. It was also commonly believed that the soul would eventually descend and reincarnate as a child in the same home or clan. This view was to have a profound impact on esoteric astrology, in that karma was carried over and depicted in the birth chart that set out a person's fate.

The concept of four Worlds and four corresponding levels within a human being is found in Kabbalah. This knowledge, it is said, goes back to the initiation of Abraham by Melchizedek, mentioned in the Bible. Melchizedek—who, it was said, had neither father nor mother, indicating that he was from the invisible zone—revealed to Abraham an esoteric teaching about the nature of Existence and its aim. This knowledge was transmitted over the generations of patriarchs but was nearly lost when the Israelites were enslaved in Egypt.

It was restated in the revelation to Moses on Mount Sinai and passed on to the priesthood. Later, it was passed on to the rabbis after

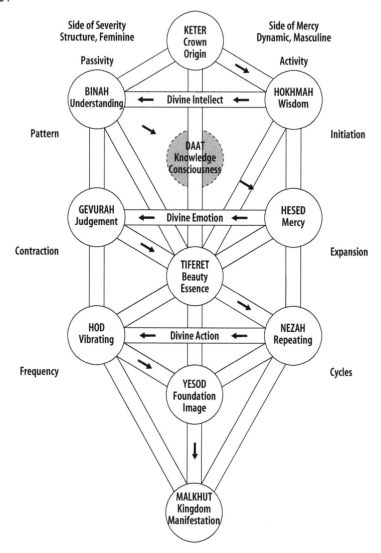

Figure 6—TREE OF LIFE

This diagram is composed of ten sefirot, or numbers, with the paths between. It is the basic model used in this book to illustrate various principles at work. The Hebrew names are traditional and taken from the Bible. Their translation is only a clue to their complex functions. The metaphysical definitions give some idea as to their qualities and capabilities. All have positive and negative aspects, like the planets. The arrows define the Lightning Flash that governs every process, be it descending or ascending. The triads are just as important as combinations of influences and flows within the circulation of the Tree. (Halevi.)

the Second Temple was destroyed. In the Middle Ages, in response to
the needs of the time, this knowledge was combined with Hellenic
and Arabic metaphysics to create a system known as Kabbalah. Let us
set out an outline of the kabbalistic view of Existence and relate it to
astrology and psychology.

The first principle is that everything came from—Nothing. This
'No-thing-ness' is seen in Kabbalah as a term for God—the Absolute.
According to tradition, 'God wished to behold God' and so out of
No-thing-ness emerged a Primal Light, symbolising Divine Will. This
radiance generated the eternal realm of all that was to come into
being. From this source emanated two complementary opposites, one
active and the other passive. They emerged out of and below the
principle of the radiant point or Crown, as it was called. In China this
trinity was known as Tao, Yang and Yin; in India they were called
Sattva, Rajas and Tamas. This triangle of primordial principles is to
be found in many other cultures. All agreed that these were the three
basic pillars of Existence. In modern scientific terms they could be
seen as the principles of equilibrium, dynamic and structure. Out of
their interaction comes an ordered diversity ranging from simplicity
to multiplicity. This phenomenon is set out in the Tree of Life and
Jacob's Ladder diagrams.

The ten principles or sefirot unfold out into a primordial pattern.
This is generated by the Lightning Flash movement from pillar to
pillar on its way down to the bottommost sefirah, called the Kingdom,
which corresponds to Earth or physical manifestation. The positions
of the planets, Sun and Moon give some idea of the character and
quality of each sefirah with Pluto posited in the space known as the
Place of Knowledge. This location, like the planet, marks the frontier
to the beyond of space and the next World.

The twenty-two paths that link the sefirot form a series of triads
which complete the archetypal model of all that is to come into
Existence. The origin of this diagram is seen in the seven-branched
candlestick in the Sanctuary of the Israelite Tabernacle mentioned in
the Book of Exodus. This has twenty-two decorations (paths) and
defines, in its form, not only the three pillars, in its right and left
branches and central trunk, but the four Worlds of Divinity, Creation,
Formation and Action in the spaces between the arms and base.

This metaphysical diagram is the figure we will use to integrate the
disciplines of astrology and psychology with Kabbalah. At this point
we are looking at the archetype of archetypes. Here is, for example,

the pattern of the Solar system. While the 'Tree' appears to be rigid it is, in fact, extremely flexible as the sefirot, paths and triads interact like the celestial bodies, the Earth, Nature and humanity.

Figure 7—ADAM KADMON
In ancient times, symbolism was the language of knowledge. Much could be summed up in an archetypal image. In this case the Holy Name, YHVH, here written in a vertical form, defines the Divine Realm of Emanation. This was called the Kavod, a vast radiant figure of fire seated upon the Throne of Ezekiel's vision. It is the place where all human beings come from as sparks of pure consciousness. It is also the model for the Zodiacal man of Astrology. Here the Hebrew letters Yod, Heh, Vav and Heh define the three pillars of the Tree of Life and the four Worlds. (Graphic by Halevi.)

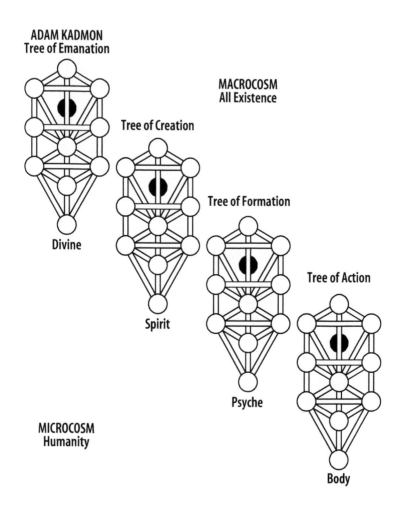

ADAM KADMON
Tree of Emanation

MACROCOSM
All Existence

Tree of Creation

Divine

Tree of Formation

Spirit

Tree of Action

Psyche

Body

MICROCOSM
Humanity

Figure 8—FOUR WORLDS
According to Kabbalah, the highest universe is that of the Divine, called
Emanation. Out of this emerged Creation, described in the Bible as the Seven
Days which set out the levels within its Tree. The third World is Formation which
corresponds to that of Paradise and the Treasure House of Souls. This is the
dimension of the psyche and astrology. At the bottom is the physical and
natural realm into which human beings are incarnated in order to fulfil their
mission. This is to aid God in beholding God, by reflecting upon Existence.
(Halevi.)

3. *Kabbalah*

The primordial World of Emanation, as it was called, contained all that would come into Existence. It was the first reflection of the Absolute in its intention to behold ITSELF. The Biblical name 'I AM THAT I AM' sets out the plan, in that the Absolute utters a sound that will extend Existence out and then echo it back from the furthest point of physical reality. The Hindu tradition calls the Word of God 'OM' while modern astronomers hear it as the faint background resonance of the Big Bang that generated the universe.

This primal realm is not God but a manifestation of the Deity. It is a cloak of Emanation that both reveals and conceals the Godhead. As such it is the place of illumination that is perceived by mystics. In Kabbalah it is defined as the sketch outline of a Divine SELF-portrait, called Adam Kadmon. This is yet to be filled in by detail, that is, the variety of Creation.

The process is symbolised by the first Seven Days or cosmic phases described in the Bible. The First Day produces Light or Fire, the Second the divisions of the firmament or Air, and the Third, Water and Earth with the first appearance of plants or Life, the principle of consciousness.

With the Fourth Day of Creation comes the ordering of the universe; that is, all the cycles and patterns that will govern Existence. Here it must be seen that the elements spoken of are at the level of Plato's realm of Ideas, not physical states of matter. The same is true of the creation of the Fowls of the Air and the Fish of the Sea on the Fifth Day. They represent archangelic and angelic principles that would maintain the dynamic and form of the universe as agents of cosmic law. The ancient civilisations saw them as the greater and lesser gods and goddesses.

Still in the realm of ideas or spirit, the Sixth Day brings forth the Beasts of the Field or the creatures that will eventually be born at the physical level. Adam, the symbol of humanity, emerges at this point as the spiritual manifestation of the Divine image of Adam Kadmon, the first reflection of the Absolute in the primordial World. On the Seventh and last Day of this cosmic octave, the creative process comes to rest.

Out of these two higher realms of Emanation and Creation emerges a third World of pure Form. Here consciousness and spiritual ideas manifest in the symbol of the Garden of Eden. Thus the essence of every mineral, plant and animal is to be seen in its pristine perfection, while the Spiritual Adam, 'male and female created He them', is divided into the form of a pair of soul mates. Adam and Eve represent the astral or psychological human entities that inhabit Paradise prior to their descent to the Earth.

Paradise is said to be particularly beautiful because it is filled with the perfect forms of all that will be manifest below in the physical realm. While this notion may seem like a fantasy to the modern sceptical mind, it should be noted that such ideals as Utopia or the noble man or graceful woman have had an enormous influence on human history and personal relationships. The belief in Paradise is more permanent than any new technology that soon becomes obsolete or empires that eventually pass away. That marvellous place over the rainbow, or beyond the sky, is as real to the modern imagination in its science fiction as it was in ancient times.

The lowest World is that of the four elements. It began, according to modern science, with a 'singularity' or point of light in the middle of some kind of space which has yet to be defined; although this 'Void' is described in many mystical teachings. Out of this first physical emanation emerged energy and matter in the form of the simplest atom—hydrogen. Here were radiance and gaseousness. Later, due to the cosmic processes set in motion, the principles of fluidity and solidity appeared to create galaxies, stars and planets. In the case of the Solar system, the Sun represented radiation and the planets various states of solid, liquid and gaseous matter. In time, the Earth coalesced into a sphere that contained all the elements. The electromagnetic field that surrounded it was the equivalent to the 'fiery' aura of a living being while the emergence of plant life indicated the appearance of consciousness on the planet.

Miracles occur when a higher realm intervenes in a lower one. This is seen every Spring when the seemingly dead earth produces a whole new generation of plants and animals, as if from nowhere. People take this phenomenon totally for granted, as they do a newborn infant with all its organs, chemistry and electronics in perfect order. Few, moreover, ever consider where the soul was before it was incarnated or why it has a particular character. This is because most people never see beyond the physical.

Jacob's Ladder sets out the scheme of four interlocked realms of Emanation, Creation, Formation and Action. In this kabbalistic arrangement, the lower part of a higher World underlies the upper section of the one below it. This allows, in the case of human beings, for the psyche to inhabit the body while having access to the universe of the spirit and the bottommost point of the Divine Tree. Unlike animals, angels and archangels, who are confined to their respective realities, humans can enter any of the four realms or be conscious of their influences. Astrology is the study of such higher influxes and their effect on the collective and individual mind.

While the four earthly elements, plants and animals are directly affected by the Sun and Moon, humanity appears also to be subject to the planets. The combination of their subtle field forces, as they move in their orbits, seems to generate a psychological climate which, though equally subtle, is just as powerful as physical weather patterns. Just as music can create moods, so the emissions of each planetary principle appear to stimulate in humanity a response that is sometimes quite dramatic. This is seen, for example, when Mars is in Aries, which can trigger conflict, sudden decisions and initiatives at both the personal and collective levels. Such a phenomenon is not unusual. The responses to radio and TV transmissions that stimulate machines to move or produce sound and images is accepted as normal. A human being is just a much more subtle receiver. People react to the frequencies emitted by the cosmic orchestra like dancers, to put it in poetic terms.

Using this ancient analogy, each of the planets has its own distinct melody. Saturn's is somewhat sober while Jupiter's is rather grand. Venus plays a seductive tune, Mercury a quickstep and Mars a sharp call. The classical gods were graphic ciphers for these celestial characteristics. The Moon, for example, was symbolised by a slender, girlish goddess or a many-breasted matron representing the New and Full Lunar stages while the Sun was depicted as a beautiful young man in his prime. As these deities moved through the musical score of the zodiacal concert, there were distinct passages in which each celestial body had its solo. Sometimes they were harmonious and occasionally they clashed as various combinations of aspects manifested, such as trines, conjunctions and oppositions, the geometric angles formed by the movements of the planets in relation to one another.

The esoteric understanding of why people respond to events in the heavens is defined by the 'as above, so below' principle. This is based upon the notion that a human being is a microcosm of the macrocosm. The concept is illustrated in Figure 9 in which the corresponding interior levels of an individual match the four universes that compose Existence. In order to gain some insight into the realms beyond the physical, we will draw on kabbalistic myth and legend to describe the nature of the higher Worlds and mankind's origin and purpose. These indicate, symbolically, the substance, structure and dynamic of other realities.

Figure 9 (Right)—JACOB'S LADDER
Here all the Trees are integrated into what is called the Fifth and Great Tree. At the lower levels are the Trees of the body and psyche. Above are the transpersonal Worlds of the archangels and the Holy Names of God. As can be seen, the bottom part of a higher World corresponds to the upper part of the World below so that they can interact. Astrology is based upon this principle, in that the World of Formation has a direct influence upon the collective and individual psyche. (Halevi.)

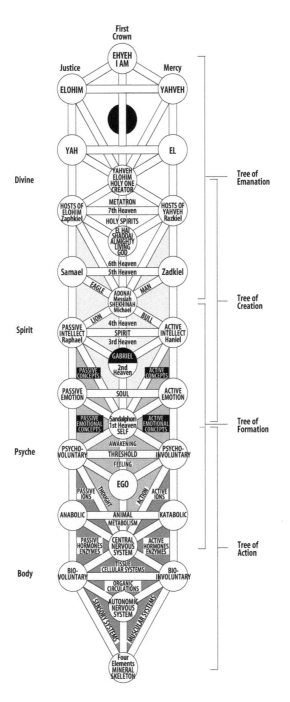

Figure 10—ZODIACAL MAN

Man as the microcosm is an image of the universe. Here he is cast in zodiacal terms with each Sign related to different parts of the body. Thus the head is ruled by Aries, the feet by Pisces. While Virgo relates to the intestines, Cancer is associated with the breasts, Leo with the heart and Scorpio with the genitals. The reason for these and other Zodiacal correspondences is that they appear to match a particular temperament and physical principle. (17th century engraving.)

4. Microcosm

According to kabbalistic legend, humanity has its origin in Adam Kadmon, the image of the Absolute. Each one of us is a cell of consciousness within this Divine being. As such, every human being has a specific position in the anatomy of this reflection of the Godhead, as part of the Divine brain, heart or other organs. That means all are involved in the process of SELF-realisation, as God wishes to behold God in the mirror of Existence. This is the purpose of our existence. At a certain point in cosmic evolution, humanity descended to the lower Worlds in order to carry out the function of being the agent of perception for the Absolute. What particular rôle each of us plays in this operation is what individual destiny is about.

It is said that as we leave the Divine realm and enter the lower World of Creation, every individual cries out 'I AM' as it becomes a spiritual entity. Then as groups, relating to specific organs of Adam Kadmon, we pass down through the seven levels of Heaven to enter Paradise or the Astral World, called the 'Treasure House of Souls' in Kabbalah. Here each male-female spirit separates out into a couple within their particular soul group. When these soul mates incarnate, they will exercise their combined gifts, after learning how to live on Earth. This may take many lives. Evidence of this is seen in talented people who clearly bring into incarnation experience and knowledge that could not be learnt in one lifetime. Every soul has a unique function, no matter how humble. Thus each individual makes a contribution to the Divine process in spite of, in some cases, one or even a series of disastrous fates.

However, before a soul can find and fulfil its destiny, it has to develop its potential. The Bible notes that Adam and Eve were in a state of innocence, and therefore they had to be taught what and what not to do before they could execute their personal, joint and group mission. The myth of the Fall was to teach humanity that the gift of free will meant responsibility, in that every action generated consequences. The resultant expulsion from Eden was not designed to

36

Figure 11—FATE AND DESTINY
Socrates, one of the world's first philosophers, although poor was a citizen of Athens. This was his fate. He could have remained a humble artisan but he chose to spend his time in intellectual enquiry, in that he asked penetrating questions during the discussions he conducted in Athens' market place. These were recorded by Plato, a thoughtful noble who used him as the model for a major philosophical treatise still studied today. This was Socrates' destiny. However, his blunt love of Truth got him into trouble and he was condemned to drink hemlock. (Socrates With His Disciples, 19th century print.)

injure but demonstrate the law of karma. The temptation of the apple was a test to illustrate that they had no one else to blame for their new situation. However, although they were now 'wearing coats of skin' or in a primitive state of being, they still retained the gift of free will and the added ability of being 'conscious of being conscious', having eaten of the Tree of Knowledge. Their descendants were to multiply and spread all over the Earth as each generation died and was reborn, along with the increasing number of new souls descending to incarnate on Earth.

Initially the various soul groups remained together as clans and tribes for many lifetimes in order to learn how to survive and work together. This was an important part of the Divine plan to train them for their destiny. In time, soul mates split up, in order to develop as individual men and women before reuniting, many lives later, as mature people. This sense of loss of the soul companion is very deep. It is one of the major preoccupations of many as they search for their original partner. This memory is represented by the animus and anima images in their psyches. However, before a reunion can occur, much has to be gone through over many lives. During these transmigrations each person acquires both good and bad karma. Generally speaking, the more advanced individuals are old souls while less experienced people have usually lived only a few lives. Eventually all the members of a particular soul group meet up again, after they have reached their optimum capacity. Together they will then develop their full potential so as to carry out their preordained mission, to aid God to behold God.

Soul groups and partners can be identified by common interests and harmonious elements in their birth charts. They will often belong to the same social level and frequently follow similar professions. This can be seen in the many great artists of the Renaissance or ingenious inventors of the 20th century. The American 'mountain men' who blazed the trails through the Wild West are a classic example of a soul group, as were the philosophers of ancient Greece. The coming together of soul mates can be seen in Saint Francis of Assisi and Saint Clare, who were clearly a couple although they never married. So, too, were the Curies, who discovered radium, and Winston Churchill and his wife Clementine, who kept him calm during the storm of War. This British Prime Minister indeed knew, from his boyhood, that one day he would have to defend Western civilisation. Upon becoming Britain's warrior leader, he observed that he had been well trained for his destiny, having been a front-line soldier and cabinet minister.

Not everybody has such an obvious or spectacular role. Many people fulfil themselves when they find their particular niche in life with the talent they have worked with over many lives. Most people have yet to find their position because they have not developed enough to be given the responsibility of their destiny. Conversely, they may have missed their opportunity or simply swum against evolution by behaving wilfully and stupidly. Such a situation can occur in quite advanced souls who choose to abuse their position. This can sometimes be seen in the birth chart of remarkably gifted people whose fate is disastrous. A multiplicity of squares or trines can indicate certain lessons have yet to be learnt. An example is the brilliant, Scorpionic US General Patton, who was contemptuous of any soldierly weakness. He had Mars square Pluto, which made him admired and feared by his own men as well as the enemy. He did not die in battle but was killed in a peacetime car 'accident', an end he would have abhorred because he cherished dying a glorious death as a brave soldier in Roman times.

Because life becomes increasingly complex as people evolve, so the birth chart of an advanced individual often contains many more factors than that of a younger soul. Fate is not always easy for those trying to develop. This is because some problem or karmic debt has to be worked out, or a particular lesson learned, which is only recognised many years later. An example of this was the gifted man who used his charm to seduce many women. He ended life alone and without an aim as he failed in his mission. His moment had come and gone unnoticed.

Over the millennia the Treasure House of Souls has been gradually emptying as more people are being born. Most begin incarnation in some remote area where the clan or village provides for and protects them, until they are ready to move on into a town or city where their horizons are extended. There they will meet the three basic human evolutionary stages. These are known as the vegetable, animal and human levels of mankind. The first stratum is primarily concerned with survival, food and sex, the second with power, wealth and fame, while the highest level consists of individuals who are trying to live an ethical life, help others and serve the Godhead.

These three types are to be found everywhere on Earth. The vegetable level is the most common in that they are the youngest and most innocent of souls. Highly competitive animal people can be seen in every dominant position from rulers of empires to leaders of criminal gangs. They are also to be observed in the sciences, arts and academia and even the priesthood. Human humans are quite rare. They are the great saints and sages of mankind, the best of creative and inventive people and finest of heroes and heroines, many of whom are unknown as they often avoid being noticed in order to execute their missions without interference.

As can be seen in Figure 9, a human being is composed of several levels. The bottommost World relates to the body's anatomy while just above is the structure of the psyche. The vegetable person lives primarily in the body and is therefore largely subject to physical conditions. The animal person's centre of gravity is midway between the influence of body and psyche while the individual trying to be fully human is in contact with the levels of the soul and spirit. Which stage of evolution a man or woman is at cannot be determined by a birth chart but what they have to develop and the pattern of their fate can be. This is where astrology and Kabbalah can come together to give a three dimensional picture, with the aid of psychology, of that individual's journey.

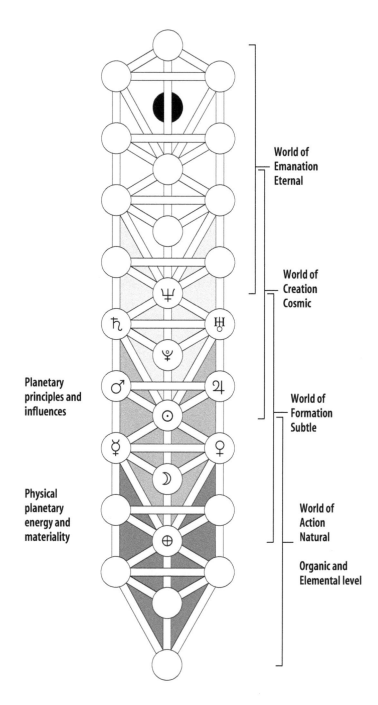

Planetary
principles and
influences

Physical
planetary
energy and
materiality

World of
Emanation
Eternal

World of
Creation
Cosmic

World of
Formation
Subtle

World of
Action
Natural

Organic and
Elemental level

41

5. Influences

cosmic 宇宙的.
terresterial 地球的. tidal. 潮期的.
tilt. 倾斜 psyche: 灵魂·心智. resonance: 共振·共鸣.

Astrology is the study of celestial conditions and their effect on humanity. It is generally accepted that cosmic forces have an enormous influence on the terrestrial environment. The various Ice and Tropical Ages, it is believed, are the result of Solar fluctuations or the tilt of the Earth changing in relation to incoming cosmic winds of radiation. It has been noted that wine quality can vary according to the Sun's cycle and that blood will coagulate quicker when the Moon is in a certain phase. Like the sea's tides, these phenomena are generally accepted.

As regards more subtle effects on the psyche and history, it is observable that the insane are more prone to agitation when the Moon is Full and that sunspot patterns relate to the world's economic productivity. Wars, moreover, often occur when Mars, Saturn and Uranus are in certain combinations while periods of prosperity arise when Jupiter, in particular, is well aspected. These facts, however, are not generally acknowledged. stagnation: 停滞.

What is being indicated is that the Solar system not only generates physical events but ever-changing psychological conditions that cause history to be a series of tidal patterns. There are, for example, periods of mass migration, high civilisation and stagnation. This raises the question: how does the cosmos influence humanity? The answer is, through the principle of resonance. If the universe is made up of energy and matter in a constant state of oscillation, then it follows that everything in it will respond to any shift in frequency. The physical world is, in reality, only an appearance of stability. Even the most

---

Figure 12 (Left)—SOLAR SYSTEM
The Solar System occupies a specific position on Jacob's Ladder. This is not the physical location but the essences of the celestial bodies. The Sun, Moon and planets, in Kabbalah, are seen as angelic beings rather than gods as the ancients defined them. This conclusion was based upon observation of the character and various effects upon people and events. Mars, for example, when in Aries, seemed to generate either aggression or hard discipline in individuals or communities governed by this sign. Seen as an astral organism, the Solar system generates a kind of cosmic weather that influences history. (Halevi.)

oscillation 振动.

42

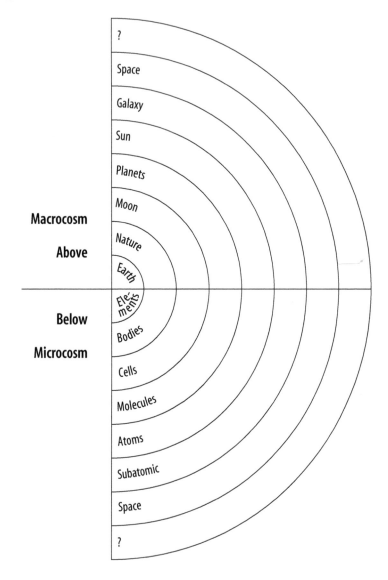

Figure 13—COSMIC INFLUENCES
The esoteric maxim 'As above, so below' is set out here in scientific terms. Each
level resonates with its counterpart. This is seen, for example, in sunspot
activity and world trade cycles while storms on Jupiter appear to disrupt
telecommunications on Earth. At a more subtle level, celestial influences likewise
affect human beings, according to their configurations and positions and a
person's birth chart. This premise is the basis of astrology. (Halevi.)

dense 稠密的 浓厚 浓稠的 affect 折磨
vibrating: 振动 Compress 压缩 紧缩
ephemeral: 短暂的

utilise 使用

dense substances are no more than vibrating forms. Indeed, according to science, even the heavy metal lead is largely composed of space. Further, if your body were to be compressed into a true solid it would occupy but a minute dot. Matter, in fact, is quite ephemeral and can be easily affected by a small fluctuation. Water, for instance, only needs a change in energy level to transform it into a solid or a gas. Similarly, a favourable Jupiter-Venus angle can make a person optimistic and enthusiastic for as long as this harmonious transit lasts, be it a day or a week. The same is so for a seemingly unaccountable depression when Saturn afflicts a person.

emit: 发出, 发射

The Sun and planets emit a wide range of subtle frequencies which stimulate distinct responses within organic life on Earth. Each plant and animal is tuned to react to particular Solar emissions. For example, this can be seen in the appearance of different flowers at certain times of the year and in the migration of birds. In the case of humanity the response is more complex, as mankind has a wider sensitivity and capability.

perturbation 扰动 不安 扰乱   neutral: 中立的

Figure 13 sets out the above-below principle that operates in the universe. Organic life on Earth is influenced by the changing balance of forces within the planet's electromagnetic field. If this is too greatly disturbed then freak weather, plagues and mass insanity occur. If the perturbation is within certain limits, then a period of activity happens that can be either creative or destructive or both, according to how humanity decides to utilise such incoming energy. These influxes from the Solar system are quite neutral.

anatomy: 解剖学

A human being is made up of physical, psychological, spiritual and Divine components. Thus while the material organism responds to local mechanical, chemical and electronic stimuli, the psyche with its more subtle anatomy reacts to a different set of frequencies. Every woman is all too aware of premenstrual tension which usually occurs when the Moon is in a particular position. Sensitive men are often conscious that they are not so energetic when the Sun is opposite or squared to their Sun sign. Moreover, many people notice that there are periods in life when nothing much happens and others when they are highly active. These latter times are when unexpected opportunities seem to open up due to cosmic conditions coinciding with seemingly unrelated circumstance. Close observation reveals that this is not the case as nothing in the universe happens by chance, according to the esoteric viewpoint.

For example, an Aries will often seek action when Mars is in his

44

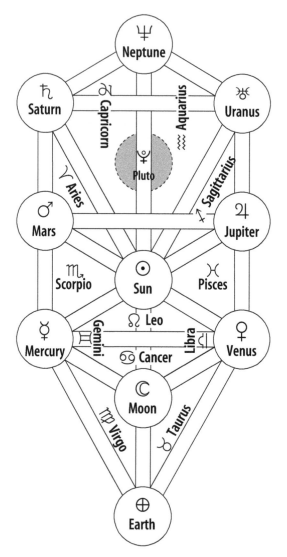

Figure 14—ASTROLOGICAL TREE
Here each celestial body and Sign is associated with a particular position in the
Tree. The rationale of the triads is that the ruler of each Sign has a triad directly
connected with it. For example, Mercury rules Virgo and Gemini, the triads of
Thinking and Intuition. The Sun and Moon occupy the triads of lesser and
greater consciousness in Cancer and Leo; while Mars and Jupiter anchor the
triad of the soul with the Sun. The great outer planets of Saturn and Uranus form,
with the Sun, the triad of the spirit; with Pluto and Neptune giving access to the
triad of the Divine. (Halevi.)

sign and when he is particularly bored with his job, while a Cancerian woman might have a compulsive desire to start a family when Jupiter is in her sign and she is approaching the end of her childbearing days. In contrast, Sagittarians could become extremely depressed when Saturn is squared to their Sun, just as they want to start a new project. These moods arise from the unconscious which is the instrument that reverberates to the current movement of the celestial concert.

The power of vibration, rhythm and tone has long been recognised and used. For thousands of years, Martial bands have caused millions to join the armed forces, Venusian love songs have been performed for centuries to facilitate courtship and seduction, while sombre Saturnian compositions have long been used to add gravitas to solemn occasions. As each member of the Solar orchestra has its solo piece or theme played, so humanity and individuals perform various ballets. Sometimes there is such a crescendo of celestial music that whole masses are stirred to break with habit and tradition and dance along with the mood of the time.

An example of this is seen in the 19th century when millions of people migrated from Europe to the New World even though they knew it would be very difficult to start a different kind of life. This collective movement was created by Neptune being in Aries squared to Uranus in Cancer. Neptune, the planet of visions and delusions, was in the sign of new beginnings and courage. It stimulated many to escape from the disruption of Uranus, the planet of radical change, at home, represented by Cancer. Throughout Europe, around this time, there was a major struggle for political reform that was thwarted by the ruling caste as Saturn, the planet of government repression, moved into Aries.

It is interesting to observe that the notes of the musical octave can be placed on the Tree of Life diagram in the Lightning Flash descent from the top. The octave is a universal pattern found in many things from the chemical table of elements to the Solar system. Neptune can be seen as the initial Do, with Re at the position of Uranus and Mi at Saturn. Pluto represents the pause or interval, with Jupiter as Fa and Mars as So. The Sun as the pivot of the Solar system is its essence and does not count as a note. La is represented by Venus and Ti by Mercury. The Moon fills the lower interval before the final Do of Earth. These musical notes are the various frequencies that resonate within the sefirotic Tree structure of the microcosm that is a human being.

If the music of the spheres influences what occurs on Earth, then it is reasonable to suppose that any entity born at a particular moment will take on the character of the time. A good example of this is the birth of a nation. Let us take the United States of America. According to one account, this came into being, at 3.04 am on the 4th July 1776 when the Sun was in Cancer, the sign of the people, and the Moon was in Aquarius, the sign of political ideals. Such a combination, together with the positions of the planets in certain signs and mundane houses, should theoretically generate a specific and unique nation. Let us examine the American birth chart to see if this is borne out.

6. *Entity*

In 18th century Europe the Enlightenment movement was at its height. Educated people were seeking new and radical solutions to an old and decaying political and social situation. For about two thousand years, the Neptunian-Jupiterian character of the Piscean Age had perceived the world almost entirely in religious terms. This had begun around 500 years Before the Common Era (BCE) with a remarkable group of advanced souls such as Pythagoras, Confucius, Zoroaster, Buddha, and Isaiah. This religious trend was continued by Jesus and Mohammed and maintained by later prophets, sages and saints. However, the Piscean Age was coming to an end around 1600, as the Renaissance and the Reformation indicated the onset of the Aquarian Age of social revolution.

These Ages are the 'months' of the great zodiacal 'year' which result from a 'wobble' of the Earth's axis which causes the point at which the Vernal Equinox occurs to regress through the zodiac. The 25,800-year cycle is not unlike an extended version of the annual Solar passage through the signs, but in reverse.

Up to the late Middle Ages, people under the influence of the Piscean Age had been preoccupied with religion. The founding of various faiths, based upon the revelations of mystics, and the development of a powerful priesthood held whole populations in awe. However, with the advent of printed books, Humanism and social science in the 15th century, ecclesiastical authority began to give way to ideas about secular matters and political issues. In the mid-17th century the terrible wars between Catholics and Protestants finally broke the by-now rigid hold of religion in Europe, as its intelligentsia began to consider how a new kind of world order could be brought into being. Here began the Aquarian Age.

In England and France radical ideals of freedom, equality and fraternity, so characteristic of Aquarius, were developed and polished. The English Civil War disposed of the Divine Right of Kings; but Oliver Cromwell, the Parliamentary leader, was just another dictator

48

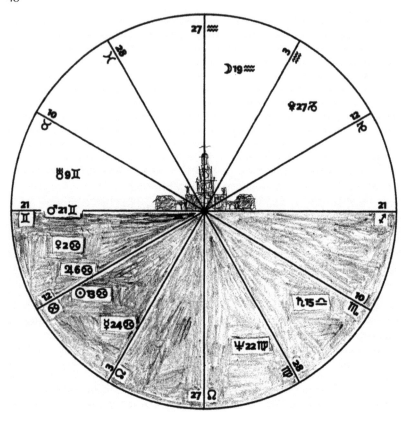

Figure 15—BIRTH CHART
The United States was born, according to some, at 3.04am on July 4th 1776 at the Philadelphia State House. This is shown as a silhouette on the skyline as Mars rises above the Eastern horizon which is at 21° of Gemini. The Midheaven is at 27° of Aquarius with the Moon nearby at 19°. The Sun and most of the other planets are below the horizon, except for Pluto and Uranus. The configuration gives the new nation a Cancerian sense of itself but an Aquarian persona. This is borne out by America's strong family orientation and its revolutionary desire to make the world in its own image. Unfortunately, Mars on the Ascendant indicates both internal and external conflict, despite its good intentions. (Halevi.)

while in France the monarchy's power was still absolute. If any great social change was to occur, it would have to be in the British North American colonies which enjoyed a freedom and prosperity unknown in the home country. This was because the migrants could acquire land or fully exploit their talents. By the late 18th century the Americans had reached a point where they could support themselves economically and therefore be quite independent from Britain. This occurred as the yet-undiscovered planet Uranus entered its own sign, Aquarius, in 1745.

When Uranus moved into Gemini in 1775, a revolt broke out in the colonies over tax without representation in the Parliament in London. The American revolution led to a Declaration of Independence and Bill of Rights based upon the social ideals formulated in Europe where they could not be implemented due to the entrenched mind-set of many centuries. So it was that a new kind of nation was born, ruled by the will of its people and not by an aristocratic establishment. This event triggered dozens of revolutions in the following centuries all over the world. It is interesting to note that Uranus was discovered in between the American and French revolutions. They mark the period when the Age of Aquarius began to supersede that of Pisces.

In the minute and hour the United States was created, the Ascendant was 21 degrees of Gemini with Mars exactly on the same spot. This said that the nation was born out of a fraternal struggle of Britons fighting Britons, as one politician saw it. It also indicated there would be strife within its community when the Ascendant and Mars were afflicted. This manifested later in the Civil War between North and South, the long campaign against the Indians and the highest crime rate in the Western world. On the positive side, Sun in Cancer in the 2nd House foretold great wealth and security for the masses. Indeed, this promise attracted millions of migrants to the country. Mercury in the same sign and House was to make America the world's financial and media centre, although a sextile to Neptune in Virgo, in the 4th House, would make it susceptible to excessive business speculation and commercialised fantasy. This was to manifest in Wall Street and Hollywood.

The Moon in Aquarius, the sign of social innovation, would make many Americans believe that their form of democracy was the best in the world, despite depriving the native Indian population and black slaves of their rights. With the Moon in the 9th House of ideals, the United States would send forth missionaries to spread the doctrine of

Figure 16—AMERICAN CIVIL WAR
In 1861, Uranus returned to its original position while Mars also transited its
own natal point. This triggered a brother-against-brother conflict over whether
the Federal government or State government should be dominant. The issue of
slavery sent the Northerners and Southerners to fight each other over principles
that split families as they fell under the negative influence of the afflicted
Geminian Ascendant. It was one of the bloodiest civil wars fought in the name of
freedom. (Union (Northern) and Confederate (Southern) armoured battleships in
the Battle of Hampton Roads. 19th century print.)

enterprise, capitalism and economic colonialism under the banner of freedom and self-determination for all. Jupiter in the 1st House gave the American character its generosity, openness and flamboyance, while Venus in the same House accounts for a preoccupation with money, beauty and sexuality. Saturn in Libra in the 5th House adds the fascination of glamour and power. This is seen in an enormous reverence for any celebrities, be they politicians, media stars or even infamous criminals.

Uranus in Gemini in the 12th House gives a sinister dimension to the American scene. Besides the huge number of people in prison (two million at the time of writing), violence was to be accepted as part of the culture. The 'right to bear arms', originally meant as a check on a tyrannical government, was to become a painful issue, with more murders committed in the country than in any other Western nation. The Cancer Sun's tendency to lunacy is both the 'kooky' and the shadow side of America. Fads and fashions are constantly emerging from this remarkably vital, innovative and open-minded society which invented the ultimate 'pop' culture.

In spite of the popular trends, Pluto in Capricorn in the 8th House gives Americans a deep spiritual hunger. They will permit anyone to practise whatever religion they wish, within reason. While this has granted tremendous tolerance, it has also allowed some very peculiar movements to come into being. Most of these were benign but some were quite sinister. It was in the USA that Spiritualism began, as did Theosophy and Christian Science. Many new cults have been spawned in the country and ancient ones adopted, such as Buddhism, Zen and even Kabbalah. The occult and astrology have vast numbers of American followers and the New Age movement of the late 20th century began in America. Pluto, the principle of transformation, in the sign of tradition and the house of the esoteric, could not but bring forth such fruit.

Like people, nations have crises. In April 1861 Uranus returned to conjoin the natal Uranus of the American horoscope while Mars conjoined both transiting Uranus and the natal Mars, before crossing America's Gemini Ascendant. During these transits the first shots were fired in the American Civil War which cost around 186,000 lives and did much damage. The issue was whether the United States would remain a unified family (Sun Cancer) or break up. After a bitter conflict in which brothers fought on different sides, the nation was forcibly held together. It was a conflict over a political principle (Moon in

Aquarius). Slavery was a secondary consideration. First came the preservation of the Union.

From an astrological viewpoint, the transits of Uranus and Mars, the planets of disruption and war, in Gemini were agitating and dividing the collective American psyche. When the warlike nature of the 1st House was activated, the tension between the Northern Puritan culture and the Cavalier South was too much to contain. Some say the participants were reincarnations of the Roundheads and Cavaliers of the English Civil War, still working out their karma as to who should rule, the people or government. Lincoln, the then US President, would not betray the ideals of the Founding Fathers because he was a Sun and Ascendant Aquarian. No one with this Fixed configuration could change his position. So the war had to be won by the Union, whatever the cost.

The United States is at present the richest and most powerful country in the world. No other nation can compete with its economic clout or the might of its military machine. American culture is imitated everywhere as the model of prosperity. It is the 'promised land' for millions at home and abroad; but whether it is a great civilisation only time will tell as nations, like individuals, can be at different levels. Here is where fate and what use is made of it brings in other dimensions.

7. *Fate*

Not everyone is necessarily a young soul at birth. It is not, as noted, uncommon for some children to be brighter than others or even brilliant with a special talent. As a child, Mozart composed music far beyond his years while others have been able to speak several languages before they were three years old. This suggests that the incarnating psyche carries within it knowledge gained in a previous existence. The implication is that the psyche is an organism that survives physical death and retains what it learned in the unconscious.

Most of humanity is either young and at the vegetable level of basic survival or slightly more mature and at the animal stage. Those at the human level are usually less concerned about security or ambition and more interested in personal or collective development. The result is that vegetable people are largely governed by the physical environment while the other two are, to different degrees, subject to celestial influences. However, the difference between the animal and human levels is that the latter can consciously control their fate and not just react to astrological transits.

Young souls instinctively seek out a safe habitat where they can nourish themselves and their offspring. They are usually dominated by their Ascendant body type or the Moon, which means they share in the general fate of their community. For instance, they will prosper when their clan or nation has Jupiter in its astrological sign or be involved in war when Mars or Pluto transits their collective Ascendant. An example of this was the mass movements of the mounted Mongol warriors in the 13th century when Pluto was passing through Sagittarius, which combines the bowman and the galloping horse in its symbol.

The psychological mechanism of this phenomenon is seen in the power of a peer group. If miners in a village go on strike, few will go against their workmates. Their identity is based upon their occupation and community and, therefore, they will not jeopardise their position for fear of losing their job and being ostracised. Survival comes

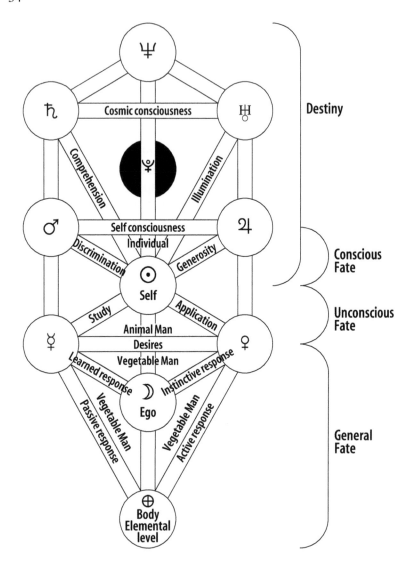

Figure 17—LEVELS OF FATE
Not everyone lives out their birth chart to the full. Most are content to exist at the levels of the Ascendant or their Moon. This means making no great effort to develop out of any situation; while those who wish to individuate seek to become masters of their fate and develop their full potential. They eventually become conscious of their destiny and use the full capacity of their birth chart. (Halevi.)

before any individuality. This phenomenon subjugates the Lunar mind-set which will not break any habit and cultural pattern unless it has to. It will therefore go along with the crowd, even if it means disaster.

At the leadership level, animal stage people are prompted to act if astrological and social conditions coincide. Many dictators, like Mussolini, can take over a whole country if the political situation is ripe and they are ready, because 'their Star' is rising. This is a symbolic way of saying that an astrological transit, favourable to them, is operating.

Mussolini, a Leo, had Uranus in his 10th House of ambition. This gave him an obsession to turn Italy into a modern Roman Empire. He came to power as the Node, Jupiter and Saturn trined his natal Moon, Mars and Saturn in Gemini in his 7th House of Partnership. This stimulated his innate eloquence to convince the Italian masses that he, Mussolini, was the political messiah they were looking for to save their chaotic country. As a nation ruled by Leo they loved the theatrical grand gesture, of which Mussolini was master. So it was that the Italian people became his audience and partners in a grand opera in which they would together recreate the Roman Empire.

This fantasy manifested not only in martial uniforms, attitudes and manners throughout the country but even in schools being turned into military academies. It was as if the whole nation had become insane as Neptune, the planet of delusion, moved through Leo. Italy invaded Abyssinia and annexed Albania in the 1930s and, in 1940, declared war on Britain and France as Pluto, the planet of nemesis and death, entered Leo. Within five years Italy was devastated and defeated. Mussolini, now fallen from his plinth, was humiliated and then executed by his own people. Disillusioned with his and their own performance, the Italians changed sides and supported their erstwhile enemies, the Allies, against the Germans. The opera had been brought to a sudden end as Uranus exactly conjoined Mussolini's Moon in the House of Partners. The marriage between them and him was over.

Many good and wise Italians left Italy or hid away as they were persecuted by the Fascist regime. This is because they knew what was really happening to their country and were a threat to Mussolini. To perceive truly can affect an individual's fate. They know what to avoid and when to move and this sets them apart from the crowd. Such an approach can only occur if a person is in touch with their inner self or Sun. Most people are quite unaware of how they are

Figure 18—GENERAL FATE
Everything in the universe has a place. The humblest peasant has a cosmic
purpose. Even a drunk in the street has a function, if only to be a warning to
others. Most people are subject to natural and social situations that sweep them
along in good and bad times. At this level they do not count as individuals but
general cells that perform ordinary functions. It is only when a person begins to
develop that they can become specialist and their fate a more advanced element
in human evolution. (Medieval woodcut.)

governed by current social attitudes and external circumstance and so they often do not perceive an oncoming event until it is too late. To be able to have such foresight is the result of much psychological work and some spiritual knowledge. This enables an individual to view a situation objectively, especially if they understand celestial conditions.

In Figure 17 the triad made up of Sun, Mars and Jupiter defines the soul while the triad of destiny is made up of Sun, Saturn and Uranus. These celestial principles are concerned with the pattern of many incarnations, that is, the line of an individual's development and their purpose in Existence. This has its origin, as said, in the kabbalistic notion that each of us comes from a particular part of Adam Kadmon, the Divine image of God. The concept that everything has a place in the universe is reinforced by the study of astrology which indicates, quite precisely, where we are in time and space and what this particular life is about.

Those who learn to manage their fate gradually realise what their specific task is. Moreover, more evolved people who already know this are around to guide them. The most advanced individuals are very rare but they are present to lead the human race along the road of evolution. Such individuals may appear as spiritual or philosophical figures, artists and scientists or indeed in any profession. However, not everyone can be or needs to be a master poet, soldier or statesman. Only a few of these are required to carry out certain missions. There are, however, many vacant rôles to be filled at every other level. As one famous teacher said: 'The harvest is great, but the labourers are few'. Everyone can contribute something to evolution. The housewife has the vital task of nurturing a family, the gardener his job producing the best fruit and flowers, and undertakers their very necessary task. Destiny is not about fame or fortune but identifying what task one is meant to execute. With this comes a deep satisfaction. Power, fame and wealth are quite transient when seen on the scale of the Divine Plan, in which even the most humble and unknown are personally acknowledged by God if they communicate in their own way with the Absolute.

An example of fate becoming destiny can be seen in the lives of the two seminal psychologists, Freud and Jung. The former was born into a Jewish family and the latter to a Christian minister's home. Both lived at a time when science was beginning to look at the workings of the mind. While ancient and medieval scholars knew much about the psyche, their terms were, by the 19th century, quite outdated. Moreover, the Piscean religious understanding of the subject was quite alien to the new Aquarian approach of science which believed the mind was a product of social conditioning and the brain.

Freud discovered, in his clinical work as a physician, that dreams gave access to the instinctive subconscious while Jung, in his investigations, uncovered the more purely psychological unconscious. These were two quite different levels. However, both established that the psyche was a well-ordered entity. Together they had reopened the door into the mind that had been shut by the materialistic and mechanistic trend of their period.

It was their destiny to make this rediscovery, although they were not fated to remain friends. Freud's Taurus Sun squared Jung's Leo Sun and they quarrelled. This reveals something about temperament and development. People of destiny are not always saints. There are degrees of fate as there are levels of humanity. Let us look at the structure of the mind in relation to astrology and the kabbalistic Tree of Life diagram in order to utilise Freud's and Jung's contribution to evolution.

8. *Psychology*

The reason why some esoteric traditions call the psyche the astral body is because it was believed to relate to the stars. This meant they were both composed of the same subtle substance, known as the Ether. This, the fifth and finest of elements, was said to pervade the universe and the physical body. The Hindu system of the chakras and the Chinese map of the etheric flows permeating the anatomy are the microcosmic versions of the macrocosmic field of the heavens. It is the interaction of the celestial frequencies within the Ether between the heavenly bodies and the human astral vehicle that affects the psyche.

In the Kabbalah, the psyche belongs to the ethereal realm of Formation. As such this fluidic level takes on a configuration of whatever is imposed upon it by the higher World of the spirit. In turn, the form that is brought into being moulds the character of the mind and the body, giving it a distinct personality. This is the basis of astrology. Figure 19 lays out the anatomy of the psyche in ancient, medieval and modern terms. This is an image of the mind in absolute equilibrium. In reality the upper and lower levels may not be so balanced, nor the pillars so straight. Moreover, the shape of the triads in an individual can be quite out of proportion while individual sefirot may be weak or strong, depending upon the configuration of the horoscope.

In a birth chart the Sun, Moon and planets, which parallel the sefirot, are loaded according to their zodiacal positions. Some are well placed, others afflicted and yet others in active or passive states. All this adds up to a very individual pattern which gives the psyche a unique character. More on this later.

First one must grasp the general principles set out by the Tree. As can be seen, at the bottom are all the instinctive, psycho-biological processes of the body, ego and ordinary mind. These correspond to the Ascendant, Moon, Mercury and Venus. The triads, made up from their connecting paths, are the functions of action, thinking and feeling.

60

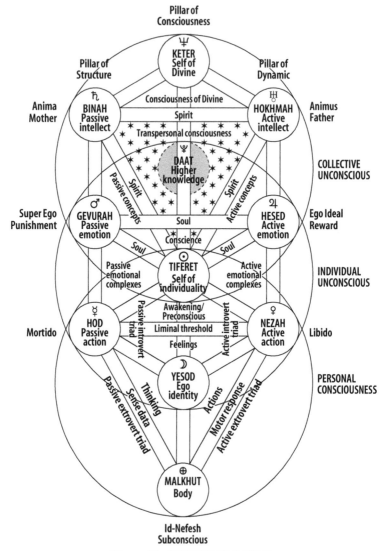

Figure 19—PSYCHE IN DETAIL

The mind is a system; like the body it is based upon Divine Laws. It has a lower automatic aspect, in which everything operates from instinct or habit. At its focus is the ego, or screen of ordinary consciousness. It is also the place where the imagination produces impressions of the inner, as well as the outer, world. Above in the unconscious are the emotional and intellectual complexes that surround the triad of the soul. Beyond this is the triad of the spirit or transpersonal aspect of the mind and the triad of the Divine present in everyone. The so-called astral body of the psyche is subject to astrological influences. (Halevi.)

Mercury is the passive mental principle that responds to situations while Venus is the active instinctive function. The Moon reflects, in its various phases, the different 'personas' of the ego, such as wearing quite different psychological faces at home, work or leisure. The libido and mortido principles represent Nature's creative and destructive drives or id, as Freud calls it. In Kabbalah this vital principle is known as the *Nefesh*.

As the Moon is the ordinary ego mind that has been conditioned by the person's culture, so the Sun represents the essential self of the individual. This sits at the centre of the psychological Tree and acts as the co-ordinator within the unconscious. As the pivot of this psychological Solar system, the self is crucial as it has access to all parts except the highest sefirah (Neptune) and lowest sefirah (Ascendant). The triads that focus upon the Sun contain all the emotional memories and ideas imbibed not only from this life but also from others. Such experiences can be either active or passive factors within the mind.

The soul is defined by the Sun, Mars and Jupiter triad. This is where conscience and free will reside between the planets of emotional contraction and expansion. Here the super ego and its complement and opposite, the ego ideal created by one's education, exercise an unconscious punishment and reward system until the development of individuation begins. Until that time the ego-Moon, with all its preset reflexes and views, dominates life.

The next level of the psyche is represented by Saturn and Uranus. These two intellectual planets form the top angles of the large transpersonal triad that has the Sun at the bottom and Pluto at its centre. Psychologically, Saturn is the principle of long and deep thought or the philosopher in the mind while Uranus is the principle of revelation and inspiration or the inner prophet. Pluto, the non-sefirah or 'dark' window, represents the mystical aspect of the mind that can acquire direct knowledge of the spiritual World beyond its veil while Neptune is the access point to the Divine realm. Neptune on the Jacob's Ladder of Figure 12 connects the psychological Crown with the lowest sefirah, or Kingdom, of the highest Tree of Emanation. As such this Neptunian position contains the psychological, spiritual and Divine aspects of the SELF of the Solar self in an individual.

Figure 20 sets out the archetypal qualities of the psychological universe of Formation. Besides the astrological principles, there are many mythical symbols from every culture that fit precisely into this

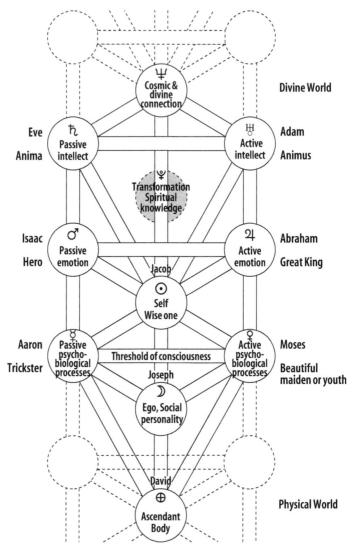

Figure 20—ARCHETYPES

The psyche is part of the World of Formation and images. These are seen in the archetypes of the mind. In this scheme, Biblical and Jungian archetypes are set on the Tree according to their psychological and sefirotic counterparts. For example, Joseph the dreamer became the prime minister of Egypt. In the psyche, this is the equivalent to the ego with the Pharaoh as the Self. Adam and Eve are clearly Animus and Anima while Jacob, the Self, was transformed into Israel when he shifted his consciousness from the psychological to the spiritual. (Halevi.)

realm of images. Figure 20, for example, illustrates some of Jung's findings which often occur in dreams. In Kabbalah, certain Biblical characters relate to particular sefirot. At the Neptunian Crown is the Shekhinah, with Adam and Eve at the Uranian and Saturnian tops of the two side columns. Beneath them come Abraham at the Jupiter position, because he loved God, Isaac where Mars is, because he feared God, and Jacob at the place of the Sun, because he experienced God. Moses and Aaron correspond to Venus and Mercury with Joseph, the Dreamer, in the place of the Moon. David, the earthy King, is at the Ascendant.

King Arthur, Queen Guinevere and the key knights of the Round Table can be set upon this archetypal Tree, as can many other legendary personalities. This is because all these symbols belong to the collective unconscious of humanity. The universal images of Mother, Father, Warrior and all the other figures common to mankind form the psychological background in the memory of nations and that of personal dreams. The individual unconscious might refer to everyday situations in a dream but they are often cast in an archetypal format that reveals what is going on deep in that individual's mind. An example is the man who dreams about being a brave soldier when he is faced with some difficult problem in his life.

Here it must be recognised that we are greatly influenced by our unconscious. Most people daydream but few realise they are being pressured or even dominated by a forgotten incident that might date back to childhood. Moreover, even more people are oblivious of any current celestial situation that might influence their mood. For instance, when Jupiter squares Mars and Mercury, people can become quite irritable or even irrational.

These planetary transits are not random but part of a programme, set up at the beginning of Time, which slowly unfolds the drama of Creation in the evolutionary path towards SELF-realisation. Each human destiny has its particular part to play in this vast cosmic process of God beholding God in the Mirror of Existence. Such a concept has given rise to a long debate about whether fate is predetermined or subject to free will. The answer is a combination of the two. While it is true that general conditions in the heavens and on Earth are fixed by universal laws, humanity can choose to go with or against evolution. However, there is a certain limitation as to what a community or individual can do within the overall scheme. The beautiful young woman can make life hell for her suitors but she will eventually grow old and lose her youthful looks and admirers.

Those who respond wisely to circumstance usually find themselves passing through life without undue stress, because they save energy wasted in a futile struggle to be different from what they are. Of course they have problems and difficult periods but these are not insurmountable, whereas those who try to live out their fantasies never find fulfilment. Intelligent and honest individuals are usually aware of the patterns of their fate. They seize every opportunity presented to them to learn more. This gives them the option to develop and exploit the potential of their birth chart. Here is where understanding one's horoscope is not just useful but vital in personal evolution.

9. *Birth Chart*

It is said that the incarnating psyche is connected to the body at the moment of conception. While this may be true, there is not much more, initially, than a fertilised cell at that point. As the embryo develops so the discarnate psyche of the individual to be born becomes increasingly drawn into physicality. Meanwhile, another process is also going on. According to Kabbalah, the person is shown, during the pregnancy, the general plan of their life to come, whom they will meet and relate to as friend, foe, relative or colleague. They will also have some idea of the major events that will happen and, most importantly, what has to be learnt or the mission to be carried out.

It is also said that as the person becomes increasingly aware of their parents to be, so they perceive the karmic connection with the family they will enter who may, for example, have been their children in a previous life. These connections are often seen in the horoscopes of families which have strong astrological aspects that interlock their fates. Those members of a family who have weak or no astrological sympathy are usually outsiders who often leave the home circle and live a very different life. Strong mutual astrological connections without doubt indicate a common karma that binds the family together until it is worked out. This may take more than one lifetime.

As the moment of birth approaches, so the embryo is increasingly invested by the incarnating psyche. This reaches a crucial point when the infant begins to move about the womb. If, for some reason, the individual being born is, for example, unwanted by a parent, this can so upset the incarnating psyche that it will impair the gestation process and a disabled child can emerge. However, while its body may be damaged, the soul is still an operational entity. Such a person then has the choice to participate in life or not. Free will can still make or mar a fate that karma has dictated. An example of this was the man born with a withered hand who was obsessed with Spain but avoided visiting the country. He may have been an inquisitorial torturer there in a previous life and not have wanted to return to the scene of his crime.

Figure 21—BIRTH
At the moment when the infant takes its first breath, the psyche changes from a
fluidic state into a distinct mind set, according to the celestial conditions. This
configuration is here being noted down by the astrologers. A birth chart is a
symbolic map of fate of the person who has come back into physical circulation.
The timing of incarnation is most important. For someone who tried to abort
their scheduled arrival, fate was out of joint. The result was that many opportunities
were missed due to a distorted sequence. (Woodcut, 16th century.)

As the moment of birth approaches, the fluidic state of the psyche begins to integrate with the infantile body. At the first breath outside the womb the psyche solidifies, like a glue does on contact with the atmosphere. It is this moment of crystallisation that sets the birth chart to respond to certain celestial frequencies. The timing of an incarnation is extremely precise because the individual has to fit into a particular niche in the scheme of history. Anyone who has witnessed a birth will know that it rarely happens according to the medically predicted time. Everything in the universe has to be in exact alignment before it can occur. This includes any caesarean operation. Such an event is part of that person's fate.

When the birth takes place, the body is immediately subject to gravity and the four elements. This moment of impact on the senses grounds the psyche as it becomes an independent organism when the umbilicus is cut. Nevertheless it is still strongly in contact with the astral realm. Infants sleep a great deal for weeks and months because the psyche finds physicality hard compared with the higher World it just came from. The first few days of life are called in Kabbalah 'the days of wisdom'. Indeed, the eyes of the newborn baby usually have the look of an adult before the demands of the body overwhelm any memory of life before birth.

From an astrological viewpoint, the sign on the Ascendant of a horoscope imprints itself on the physique of the person. Over time, this form modifies any family or racial character. Thus a person who is physically inclined to be fat, because of family genes, can be slimmer than a brother or sister, because they have a Fiery Aries Ascendant which burns off excessive fat. Likewise, someone from an athletic clan might put on weight with a Cancer Ascendant as the body slowly fills out a Watery elemental physique upon becoming an adult.

While the Ascendant is an important factor, there are other influences that can affect the body, such as Solar, Lunar and planetary aspects. These can alter, for example, the figure of a genetically thin girl with a strong Venus aspect. While she may be very skinny, a Libra Ascendant would make her extremely sexy, as some current fashion models are. Conversely a well-built lady with the same Ascendant might be very attractive to men who adore statuesque women. The Ascendant would also affect a person's facial features and body language as well as the way they react to the world physically. A Capricorn Ascendant does not like heat whereas a Leo one feels quite at home in high summer.

Figure 22—HOROSCOPE

This is the pattern of an incarnation. The ascendant indicates a Saturnine physique that will mature and age very slowly. The Sun in Capricorn in the 12th House suggests an introvert disposition while the Moon in Gemini in the 5th House means, however, they will have a public persona. The life to be lived will be much influenced by Mars, Jupiter, Neptune and the Moon's descending Node in the 7th House of Partners, indicating complex relationships. This was borne out over a long life. Indeed, the chart painted a picture of what came to pass. Such knowledge is given to us by Providence. (Halevi.)

The Tree of Life diagram gives an overall picture of the character of an individual. For instance, if all the planets on the right-hand, Yang pillar are in passive signs, such as Venus in Virgo, Jupiter in Capricorn and Uranus in Taurus, then the dynamic side of the psyche will be restrained or even frustrated. Similarly, if the planets of the left-hand, Yin column are all in active signs, one would expect such a person to be innovative but controlled in their enthusiasm.

Further, the aspects between the celestial bodies reveal the eases and tensions within the Tree. For example, Venus opposed or square to Mars would manifest in a continuous battle between passion and discipline while Saturn trine Uranus might produce an original thinker. However, Jupiter in Pisces, afflicting this configuration, could make the person's ideas somewhat confused or excessive in their suppositions. Here we see how the structure of the psyche can be emphasised, neutralised or even distorted by the configuration of the horoscope.

If the positions of the houses are logged in, alongside the placing of the planets or luminaries, then the particular way the psyche operates in relation to the outside world can be seen very clearly. For example, a chart with Saturn in Gemini in the 12th House could incline the individual to become a solitary bookworm exploring every kind of philosophy. However, if Saturn in Gemini were in the 5th House, then the person might be a popular lecturer or writer on such subjects. Again, if Saturn was in the 2nd House, then the subject might have the finest collection of antique philosophical books which would be regarded as possessions never to be read but bought and sold for profit.

When looking at the chart from a kabbalistic viewpoint, the triads, for instance, become very important. Take that of the soul. It is possible to ascertain its strengths, weaknesses and peculiarities by examining the positions and aspects of Mars, Jupiter and the Sun. This would give an insight into how an individual makes significant choices in his life, as the soul is the agent of free will. Mars in Capricorn in the 11th House would make the person somewhat socially conservative and be very selective about whom they might work with and marry. Such decisions would indeed be fatal and determine a particular quality of life.

The relationship between the Sun and Moon is crucial as they are at either end of the path on the Tree that stretches between the ego and the self. If, for example, there is a disharmonious angle, then one would expect a certain sense of confusion between the person's ego consciousness and unconscious. Sun in Libra, trine to Moon in Gemini, however, would give an individual a fluency of mind that could be a little too glib. If the Moon was in the 7th House, then the person could become a very successful lawyer and if in the 12th, a prolific daydreamer. This particular path between the Sun and Moon is known as that of 'Honesty'. It is one of the most important connections in the Tree-chart.

From these few examples it can be seen that much can be gained by putting the horoscope on the Tree. Every position and aspect affects the balance of the psyche and this leads to a deeper understanding of why temperament is the key to fate. A heavily loaded left pillar cannot but be restrained while an opposite emphasis will create an enthusiastic optimist. Whether they are good or intelligent is another matter.

10. *Incarnation*

Conception does not occur at random. Many couples try to conceive but nothing happens. On the other hand, sometimes those who have taken every precaution to avoid pregnancy do conceive. This indicates that incarnation is not just an organic process. Indeed it requires the higher Worlds of the psyche and spirit to co-ordinate with physicality before a pregnancy can be obtained. While being born may seem a random event it is, as noted, a very precise operation.

Animals are not subject to karma as they do not have free will. They are governed by instinct and general evolution. They do not incur any reward or punishment for they have no idea of morality, being entirely subject to natural law. However, every human being, having an individual soul and free will, does have a degree of choice, within limits. This means their actions, feelings and thoughts can lead them to be, as the Bible says, 'higher than the angels or lower than the beasts'. A study of human history reveals that this is the case. Adam and Eve learned, in their first lesson, that consequence follows every intention, decision and deed. This is the esoteric meaning of 'an eye for an eye and a tooth for a tooth'. In other words, karma. Out of every event involving human activity comes a physical, psychological and spiritual result that determines the kind of fate to be lived, not only in the next life but even further on.

At death, according to most esoteric traditions, there is a form of assessment by the soul of its performance in the light of objective reality. This judgement the soul cannot deny, for death is the moment of Truth. Thus each individual experiences a playback of their life without any softening of the facts. This is perceived as a mixture of ecstasy or agony as the individual views every detail of his performance. It is not the aim of this book to examine what happens in the postmortem period but to consider the prenatal epoch when the psyche begins its descent again into matter.

If the individual still has lessons to learn, then they inevitably return to Earth, pulled down by the gravity of unfinished business.

72

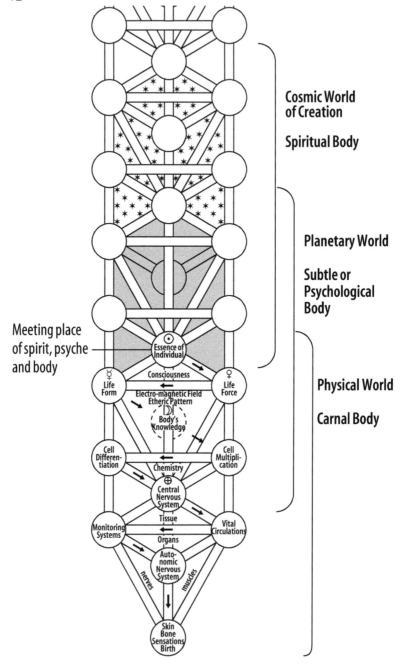

Cosmic World
of Creation

Spiritual Body

Planetary World

Subtle or
Psychological
Body

Physical World

Carnal Body

Meeting place
of spirit, psyche
and body

Essence of
Individual

Consciousness

☿ Life
Form

♀ Life
Force

Electro-magnetic Field
Etheric Pattern

☽ Body's
Knowledge

Cell
Differen-
tiation

Cell
Multipli-
cation

Chemistry

⊕ Central
Nervous
System

Tissue

Monitoring
Systems

Vital
Circulations

Organs

Auto-
nomic
Nervous
System

nerves

muscles

Skin
Bone
Sensations
Birth

Only those rare individuals who are entirely free from karma can choose whether to incarnate or not. Most people are drawn back into the flesh by an attraction or affinity with a particular place and certain circles of people, because of familiarity or unresolved issues. For example, many will inevitably wish to return to their families, their professions, friends and even enemies. Indeed, whole soul groups will gather together into the same timeframe so as to deal with specific problems, develop further or carry out some collective mission.

The organisation of such a vast operation is largely regulated by general law, like the migration patterns of animals, but within this scheme there are fine adjustments. One instance is that a particular individual needs to be born into a special circumstance, such as a musical family, while another might want to grow up in an obscure location until they are ready for their destiny. In most cases great souls have to be positioned very carefully in time and place so as to be physically mature and present at an expected historic moment. President Abraham Lincoln was at just the right age and level of experience to prevent the United States from splitting apart. History might have been quite different had he not been.

It is not uncommon for the couple seeking to conceive to be aware of a third presence with them while making love. Sensitive people are sometimes aware of a face or form of a human being hovering over them. In Kabbalah this is called the *Zelem* or the etheric image of the individual about to be incarnated. Gestation proceeds according to the Lightning Flash coming down from where spirit, psyche and Nature meet at the Crown of the physical Tree (see Figure 23) and the psyche slowly invests the embryonic body.

After birth this process continues in a growth pattern that follows an ascending Lightning Flash sequence. This is described in Shakespeare's seven ages of man. In Kabbalah there are ten phases. The Earth at the bottom of the Tree equals the elemental body while the Moon represents infancy, Mercury childhood and Venus adolescence. The Sun is seen as physical maturity, Mars early middle age, Jupiter

Figure 23 (Left)—GESTATION
Conception occurs at the meeting place of the Worlds of Creation, Formation and Action, if it is willed by the Divine. It happens if it is vital for a soul to enter the stream of evolution at a specific moment, so as to gain the most experience possible and learn the next karmic lesson. This requires careful timing so as to key in with others of their soul group, be it in a particular family, occupation or community. Once gestation begins, the psyche is loosely attached to the embryo until they fuse together at the moment of birth. (Halevi.)

74

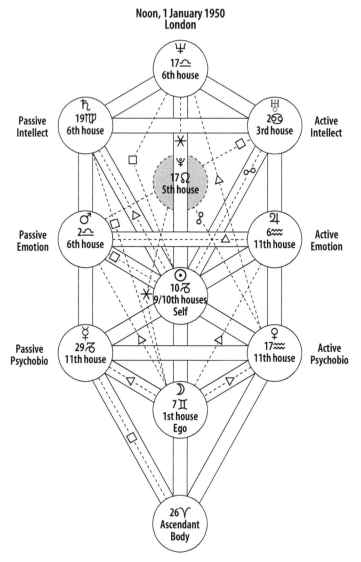

Figure 24—CHART ON THE TREE
Here the signs and Houses have been placed in the appropriate sefirot. These relate to the various functions of the psyche and give an insight into its loading. The dotted lines of the aspects supply information about various emphases within the mind. The Ascendant, Sun and Moon are key factors while the planets beyond Mercury and Venus are mainly concerned with the unconscious. Mars, in this case, in Libra in the 6th House could trigger a psychosomatic illness rooted in distress over being chronically indecisive. (Halevi.)

late middle age with Saturn and Uranus as early and late old age. Neptune is viewed, at the Crown, as death or completion of that life. Pluto, the non-sefirah, relates to any age in which a knowledge of other realities comes to the person.

This Plutonian principle is also associated with recalling life before birth and knowing something about the future. According to kabbalistic tradition, the state of higher consciousness experienced in the earliest years of life is often forgotten until the prophetic faculty is reawakened, sometimes as the result of a Pluto transit.

As people mature so the body takes on not only the form of a full-grown person but also the character of their psychological composition. This corresponds to the configuration of the birth chart. Figure 24, for example, with all signs, houses and some aspects filled in, will generate a distinct individual whose fate cannot be blamed on anyone else. In this case, it is the Tree-chart of an imaginary person we shall call Alex. This will demonstrate the interaction of the three disciplines of astrology, Kabbalah and psychology. The horoscope is set, for convenience, for noon on January 1st 1950 in London. From this we can discern something about how Alex may look, the kind of temperament he might have and what sort of fate he will possess.

With Aries on the Ascendant and Moon in Gemini in the 1st House, one would expect to see a physically small but alert man with a sharp mind. However Sun in Capricorn, on the cusp between the 9th and 10th Houses, would make Alex ambitious but cautious in his approach to life. The Capricorn, Gemini and Aries combination of the thinking triad would make him very articulate while Venus, which governs the action triad sign, could make him a little erratic in his performance by being in Aquarius. The same could be true of the feeling triad with its Gemini Moon. Fortunately, Mercury is in Capricorn which would slow the love of excitement down.

In contrast, the favourable trine between Mars and Jupiter of the soul triad would grant a certain emotional balance which, however, would occasionally be offset by Mars square the Sun of the self. This might be mitigated by the Moon trining Mars and Jupiter, which are concerned with emotional control and expression. Such a combination would give Alex a certain confidence despite a tendency to misjudge situations because of Mars in Libra. With Saturn in Virgo in the 6th House, Alex would think that being a workaholic was the norm. However, this might also be due to Uranus in Cancer in the 2nd House, making him reluctant to go home. He would feel uncomfortable there, either because he does not like being on his own or because whoever lives with him makes him feel insecure. Here we can see the contradictions that can occur in the psyche.

Alex's unconscious ambition, based upon Neptune in Libra in the 6th House, would to be the great deal-fixer. He might pursue this in business, government or as a professional counsellor. With Pluto in Leo in the 5th House, he would seek to make a reputation as a harmoniser. Unfortunately he would only gain recognition after many years. This is due to his being a Capricorn: they tend to mature very slowly. As a young man he would not be taken seriously until he gained the Saturnian gravitas of early old age. Such an achievement is not, however, automatic, as Alex may choose to remain a vegetable-level man.

Another factor to consider is that of class and culture. Alex, if he had been born in Soviet Russia, could have become a party official or, if incarnated in rural Africa, a respected tribal elder. If the chart were for a woman, say, called Alexandra, she might become the administrator of a big London teaching hospital or, if born in America, an executive in a large pharmaceutical company. If she were not at the animal level, we might find her as a village chemist in Poland or a street cleaner in China. If she had reached the fully human psychological stage, she might be a writer or philosopher concerned with the present and past attitudes and techniques of therapeutics.

The outer manifestations of a birth chart are significant, for they indicate the field in which the individual has to play out their karma. The only difference between a peasant and a president is whether their crucial decisions will affect their family or the nation. Alex may be born into a poor home and Alexandra a rich one but both, with the same birth chart, will face similar situations despite their different social or economic positions. Alex might succeed and Alexandra fail to meet the challenge of their fates, or *vice versa*. This cannot be seen in a horoscope as it belongs to the critical area of free will.

A horoscope defines what sort of life a person lives. How an individual uses their circumstance is up to them. If they choose to develop, whatever their situation, then all the levels of the chart come into operation to help them evolve whatever potential they have. This is summed up by the proverb 'Fortune favours the brave'. To ignore the possibilities inherent in the birth chart and only live off the Ascendant or Moon means that a person is subject to the fate of their family and community. For example, many people in Nazi Germany accepted this evil regime by going along with Hitler's policy. Most cheered the German victories at the beginning of the war but then had to face the result of defeat as they were inevitably caught up in their nation's fate. Few families escaped death and destruction. The same occurred in Napoleon's France where nearly all the tall men were killed in action as soldiers in his crack regiments.

Those individuals who seek to live off their Sun can escape such collective disasters, because Providence creates opportunities which only those who are psychologically awake will notice. Many people left Germany when Hitler came to power because they saw what was coming. At the personal level, close observation of the natal horoscope and current astrological conditions indicate, often quite clearly, a storm or calm coming up. The key is to be prepared for this or any event. That is how one becomes master of one's fate.

78

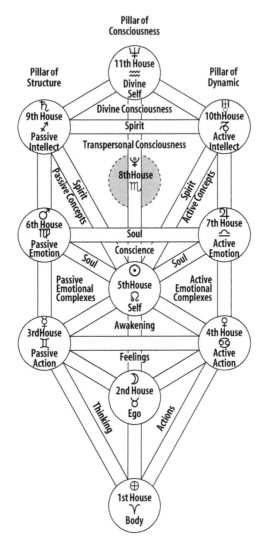

Figure 25—SIGNS AND HOUSES
*In this diagram we have simply used the sequence of the zodiac to demonstrate
principles. Thus the Moon is in Taurus in the 2nd House and so on up the Tree.
This shows how the celestial bodies are assigned a particular section of the sky,
according to the Mundane House system. This emphasises the various combinations
that make up the chart, making the ego, for example, sensuous, material and
Fixed. The Sun, here in Leo in the 5th House of the Self, would make such a person
charismatic, generous, arrogant, noble or self important. How the individual
would choose which qualities to cultivate would be where free will came into
play. (Halevi.)*

11. Lower Face

The Tree-chart of Figure 25 is a demonstration model. It could not exist in reality as it is set out according to the zodiacal sign sequence and house system, for convenience, not a specific time or place. Starting with Aries on the Ascendant, representing the 1st House, the Moon is in Taurus in the 2nd House with Mercury in Gemini in the 3rd House and so on up through the Lightning Flash of the sefirot, to finish with Neptune in the 11th House at the Crown. Pisces and the 12th House are not included as their transcendent qualities relate to the next higher realm. Nevertheless the Tree-chart will illustrate the principles to be outlined.

As can be seen, there are many cross-connections. The Sun, for example, is square to the Moon (we are not concerned with degrees in this exercise), indicating a conflict between a Fixed and Fiery self and an Earthy, Fixed Moon. This would manifest, because of their positions in the 5th and 2nd Houses, as struggle between wanting to be a charismatic leader and desiring comfort without too much effort. In this case it is the main lesson of the life. The other angles within the chart define the general disposition of the psyche. Here there are three Cardinal signs on the right active pillar, three Mutables on the left passive pillar and a full complement of the four elements in the central column. All this adds up to a very lively, contradictory temperament.

In Figure 26 the upper part of the Tree is blacked out, as for most people this is the unconscious region of the mind. Only the lower 'face', as it is called, is meaningful for many. This is the area of the ego-Moon and the ordinary mind as it interacts with the body and external world. The lowest sefirah or Ascendant corresponds with the body which is obviously partly influenced by the physical constitution. Here the Cardinal Fire sign of Aries would manifest in a dry skinned, active body, no matter which ethnic group the person belonged to.

While the Ascendant gives this subject a certain vitality, there are other modifying factors. An individual can be a muscular mesomorph,

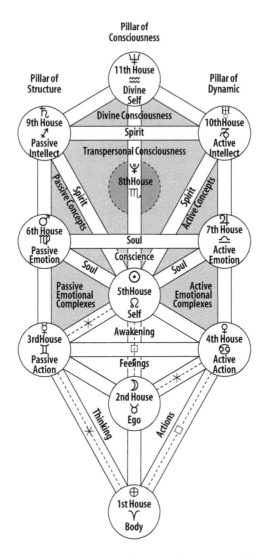

Figure 26—ANIMAL AND VEGETABLE LEVELS
The darkened part of the Tree, for animal and vegetable people, is largely unconscious and therefore has little direct influence. For them the ego is almost automatic, due to conditioning and instinct. However, animal people are proactive because they are relatively awake to their surroundings. As regards aspects, in this case Venus in the 4th House squared to the Ascendant would make the ego very resistant to change, even if the subject were a wanderer, as indicated by Mercury in the 3rd House sextile to the Aries Ascendant. He could be an entrepreneur who always travelled first class, for example. (Halevi.)

a plumpish endomorph or even a slender, nervous ectomorph. These physical characteristics relate to the action, feeling and thinking triads or body types on the Tree. The Aries mesomorph would be hyperactive, the Aries endomorph somewhat moody while the Aries ectomorph would endlessly come up with new ideas. In another person, a Cancer Ascendant would always seek to protect itself physically, feel emotionally safe only with its own kind or endlessly think up security schemes and systems. With each sign on the Ascendant an appropriate active, feeling or thoughtful manifestation would be generated according to its zodiacal character. These astrological-instinctive patterns should be taken into account.

The Moon with its changing face or persona is greatly influenced by what sign it is in. If in Gemini the features will have a sharp, Mercurial cast, while a Capricorn Moon would give a Saturnian, heavy look. In the case of Pisces, the face will have a Neptunian, fluidic quality, while a Leo Moon would be of a Sunny countenance. These are the astrological masks people wear that will process every experience according to its zodiacal nature. Thus, for example, someone with an Aquarius Moon often likes to be different, those with a Virgo ego are interested in precision. In contrast, a Libra Moon relies on charm while a Scorpio ego prefers to penetrate everyone and everything. In the case of this exercise Tree-chart, the Moon in Taurus will make the person a pleasant but relentless operator. Having the Moon in 2nd House they might well spend a lifetime collecting beautiful and expensive objects. However, if they had a 3rd House Moon, such a person might consider business or scientific data as valuable possessions. If the Taurus Moon were in the 10th House, then acquiring position in the world would be very important. The crucial point here is that the ego is largely governed by the sign and House the Moon is in.

The dark side of the Moon also has to be considered. This is the shadow aspect of the ego where the negative face of a sign and House manifest. With a Capricorn Moon one can expect vengefulness masked by a righteous sense of justice, whereas a Sagittarius Moon's hidden side might be seen in idealistic fantasies. Most people are quite unaware of this sinister aspect of their ego, although anyone with any insight will recognise the subconscious calculation of the Cancer Moon, the Leo delusion of grandeur and the double-dealing of the Gemini persona.

The ego is also greatly influenced by Venus and Mercury which represent a psycho-biological combination that affects the ordinary mind. In this chart Mercury is in its own sign and House and would, therefore, motivate the person to think out every possible angle of a situation and how to exploit it. Fortunately, this tendency would be steadied by the Taurus Moon which would slow down and check any risky or dubious scheme. Venus in Cancer in the 4th House of this Tree-chart would, with Mercury, enhance the feeling triad with its Wateriness. This would also make the person extremely sensitive, with a strong intuitive and psychic capacity. Such abilities would stimulate the triad of Awakening just above in the Tree, headed by the Sun. An example of this would be a gifted but neurotic poet who drank too much and yet could fix a piece of broken china and work a computer when he was sober.

The Leo Sun, at the centre of the Tree and on the edge of the unconscious because it is in the 5th House governed by Leo, would give the individual a strong sense of self-importance and confidence. This could be real, if a solid upbringing as well as a sound education had been absorbed by the Moon. If not, the person might be led into believing that they are a very special someone who could become whatever they wished, like the girl who believes she will be a Hollywood film star or the boy who is convinced he will, one day, be a leading statesman. Neither in fact may have the talent, stamina or the opportunity to achieve these aims. The true nature of the Sun can easily be eclipsed by such Lucific aspirations, if ambitions are more than youthful daydreams. Around the age of thirty, when Saturn returns to its natal position, most people realise what is and is not possible and accept it. Those who do not remain 'fixated' in an internal fantasy while they live everyday life. The fictional characters of Walter Mitty or Billy Liar demonstrate a quite common psychological phenomenon of secretly living their illusions.

Vast numbers of people prefer this acceptable form of lunacy because it saves them from any practical or psychological effort. The escapism of TV, cinema and sport are an outlet for the frustrated energy that is not used up. This craving for excitement, sex and violence is the result of the Ascendant, Moon, Mercury and Venus not being able to function in an evolutionary progression. As a result, a cycle of repetitive actions and lives goes on until the pattern is broken.

In the case of those who have lived a number of lives and learned to move on, there is a shift in consciousness from the lower face to its peak at the Sun at the centre of the Tree-chart. This can be activated by a Solar or planetary transit which will precipitate an opportunity or crisis. Such moments or periods of intense activity open the door to development but not everyone takes up the option and many miss the chance to develop. One instance was the teacher who endlessly complained about the way his college was run. However, when offered the job of becoming its head, while a particularly heavy transit was shaking his chart, he turned the job down. In doing so he rejected a unique possibility and missed his moment of destiny. He soon went into decline and eventually became insane because he realised he had failed what his fate had prepared him for in all his years at the college.

Assuming our artificial example is a man, whom we shall call Peter, let us examine his soul triad, made up of Sun in Leo, Mars in Virgo and Jupiter in Libra. This psychological organ is vital as regards every fatal decision. With Mars in Virgo, his judgement would be inclined to be very exacting and self-critical, in contrast to his Jupiter which would be somewhat lax. This would generate great emotional conflict as Mars in an Earth sign does not relate to the Jupiter in an Air sign or the Fiery Leo Sun. As there is no Water in the soul triad, Peter would have to rely on his Venus in Cancer or instincts for any feelings about anything serious. This could cause problems, especially as regards women, for he might not be able to tell the difference between emotion and passion. This could wreck his love life. Any potential partner would not know what was going on, as his actions and attitudes would be quite confused as regards a serious or casual sexual relationship.

When the structure and dynamics of a horoscope are put on the Tree, much can be seen about how the various psychological functions interact. Certain patterns can be identified very clearly. However, whether Peter acts as a vegetable person, an animal individual or a mature human being is of critical significance. All these levels are present in everyone. For most people the unconscious is far beyond the ordinary mind and so they act largely out of the lower face of habit. Nevertheless, what lies outside ego and even a degree of Solar self-consciousness does have an unseen influence, like the planets and stars in daytime.

12. Unconscious

The unconscious lies beyond the liminal threshold made by the path between Mercury and Venus. For much of the time people are only aware of what is going on immediately around them. If, as sometimes occurs, an event wakes people up psychologically, they see a different kind of world. Things are much sharper to the senses and there is a curious awareness of being a watcher. By this is meant observing from the Sun of the self rather than the ego or Moon. Those at the animal stage of development cultivate this experience, as it gives them an edge in any competition. While it enables them to outwit rivals, it also opens an insight into the unconscious and access to the soul. Most animal people ignore this opportunity because they are still driven by their compulsion to compete but some, in time, begin to be reflective, like the pop star perceiving that his fame is ephemeral or the business woman who realises success does not bring happiness.

Everyone, to a greater or lesser degree, is influenced by their unconscious. This contains all the experience of this life and other incarnations. The hidden part of the mind also holds all the attitudes of a person's culture in the form of the super ego and the ego ideal. These are the negative and positive models of how not to, and how to behave. Nevertheless, despite such conditioning, ancient memories persist in many people. Some, for example, fear water or heights because they were drowned or fell to their death in a previous life. Then there are those who are fascinated or repelled by a certain country or period in history. While such phobias and preoccupations can be explained as psychological fixations, they are more often than not connected with overlaid memories, which have left an indelible imprint. Ordinarily people are unaware of this phenomenon but they are still influenced by it. Astrologically such factors can be found in the 8th and 12th Houses of a horoscope where perhaps Neptune, Saturn or Mars are placed under pressure by aspect. Neptune conjunct Saturn in Pisces in the 12th House might be the result of a long time in a mental asylum or having been a nun for many centuries.

The super-ego-ideal can be greatly influenced by what astrological configuration a person has. Someone with Mars in Aquarius might seek to break every rule while another with Jupiter square to Saturn may be quite intolerant. An example of Saturn conjunct Venus in Taurus is the puritanical man who sees sex everywhere, while a Venus trine Jupiter in Libra in the 5th House might stimulate such delight in sensuality that a girl becomes a libertine despite being brought up in a Puritan clan. Here one would suspect that there was some family karma being worked out.

The super-ego-ideal, which is made up of the planets on the two side pillars of the Tree-chart, dominates both the animal and vegetable levels of people, be they desert nomads or sophisticated city dwellers. Even the hardened criminal will not break the ego ideal rules of the Mafia which tell him what he can and can't do. The same is true for the university professor who must abide by academic etiquette or he will not be considered for promotion. Indeed, society has to be based upon a set of do's and don'ts or it would fall apart. As it happens, this concurs with the laws of Nature which are primarily concerned with managing large numbers. In the case of those who wish to individuate, a conscious effort is required to free the psyche from the dominance of cultural habit and employ Nature to aid personal development.

Let us take our example of Peter and his Tree-chart. He has Mars in Virgo, which would make his super ego somewhat fussy, while his Jupiter in Libra in the 7th House would long for the ideal of having a beautiful wife and home. This could create problems as few women would be perfect enough for his anima image, generated by Saturn in Sagittarius in the 9th House. He would expect her not only to be lovely but also lively and clever to match his Mercury in Gemini in the 3rd House. All this would be an unconscious set of criteria in seeking out a socially acceptable partner.

With Sun in Leo in the 5th House, Peter might assume that his dream was the norm, until the women in his life and male competitors showed him otherwise. At the age of about thirty, during his Saturn return, he would have the choice of facing reality or preferring fantasy. If he took the latter he could finish up, with his Moon in Taurus, as a mangy Lion and bar-room braggart who hated the woman he bedded.

If he decided to relate to the real world, he would then have to deal with all the habits and attitudes he had acquired and rework them, together with the balances and imbalances set out by his Tree chart.

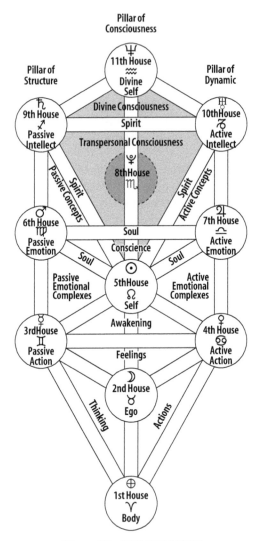

Figure 27—HUMAN LEVEL
Here the individual is aware of his interior processes which requires a degree of Sun-Self consciousness. Such a person would know, for example, that with Mars in Virgo in the 6th House he would be excessively critical. This would affect the passive emotional triad with a crippling fear of falling short of perfection, especially with Sun in Leo in the 5th where only the best will do. This could stimulate a depressive inclination that would have to be worked on to keep a balance. Jupiter in the 7th in Libra could alleviate the problem through a loving companion but it would be hard labour for the partner. Here we see how a particular fate is generated. (Halevi.)

This would require taking into account his active and passive emotions and concepts as tuned by the side pillar planets. For example, he must restrain his Martial tendency to be too critical and check his Uranus in Capricorn tendency to be contradictory in his chosen profession. This would probably be some large political or commercial organisation in which he wanted to become, as a Leo, a leading light with noble Sagittarian aims. All this would be possible, if he were psychologically awake and living off his Sun. If not, as is usually the case, Peter, governed by his upbringing and the mood of the times, would fantasise about his ambition until he realised it was never going to happen. He would then go into decline as a Lion who had lost his pride and ambition.

However, should he succeed in becoming the head of a department, he would express himself in compulsive and erratic actions, emotions and thoughts. Indeed he might turn into a little Napoleon, asserting his power with ruthless charm. If he were allowed to get away with it, he would become totally identified and obsessed with his rôle, until some other animal person with bigger teeth defeated and ousted him from a job only one individual could hold. This event, probably precipitated by a Uranus-Mars transit, might wake Peter up and make him consider his mistakes instead of plummeting down.

Such a moment of self-consciousness, no doubt stimulated by a transit of the Sun, perhaps also by Uranus, opens up the option of choice. Here the other components of the soul triad, Mars and Jupiter, would come into play even if they were not directly involved in the incident. It is an awareness at the soul level, the human dimension of an individual, that can make a fatal decision. Often years later we remember such turning points with satisfaction or bitter regret as we realise that the soul foresaw exactly what was at issue. Those who choose to listen to their conscience usually fare better in their fate than those who ignore its advice.

The spiritual dimension of Peter's life, according to his chart, is concerned with ordered inspiration due to Uranus being in Capricorn, Saturn in Sagittarius and Pluto in Scorpio. The Sun in Leo in the 5th House could take all these combinations and indeed transform Peter into a remarkable leader, if he chose to develop himself. As his Uranus is in the 10th House, his Saturn in the 9th and his Pluto in the 8th, he might be a public figure who was known to many people as an unconventional philosopher or radical religious minister. Meister Eckhart, the medieval priest who was also a mystic, is an example. He filled the church every Sunday because of his inspired sermons and writings, much to the annoyance of his politically ambitious, animal level archbishop.

The zodiacal positions of Saturn, Uranus and Pluto mark out a particular generation. Many who fought in the first Great War had Pluto in Gemini, being born in the 1890s. This association of the planet of death with the sign of youth was borne out by the destruction of the flower of that generation on all sides. In contrast, the 'Flower Children' of the 1960s had Pluto in Leo. Here the positive regenerative aspect of the planet expressed itself in an exotic popular culture. With Uranus in Gemini, for those born just after the Second World War in the 'Baby Boom' generation, experimenting with sex and drugs upon becoming young adults was quite the fashion. Saturn entered Virgo in 1949 and this generated a great interest among young people in the 1960s and 70s in ancient medicine and personal health and development. All these factors were in the character of that era.

Neptune in the Tree-chart represents what a person worships. In this case of Peter, with the planet in Aquarius in the 11th House, he would devote his life to social change. This belief would unconsciously filter through to draw him into protest politics, alternative religion or 'Green and organic' industry. If he were at the vegetable level in Soviet Russia, he would have become a devout Communist; if at the animal stage, a committed dissident against a failed Marxism. If he lived in the United States he might, as a 'common person', as the ancient Greeks called them, be just an ordinary 'guy', and if an 'uncommon man', a smart entrepreneur making big money. However, if he were at the human level of a 'hero', he could be an eminent social commentator for the media or Black leader like Martin Luther King. As can be seen, destiny is a combination of the birth chart, level of development and external circumstance.

13. *Circumstance*

Human evolution within the Divine Plan takes many forms. This is partly determined by the outer planets of Saturn, Uranus, Neptune and Pluto, which influence the character of succeeding epochs. Most people, in each generation, are in fact their own ancestors carrying over their personal and collective experience and karma. The rest are young or new soul groups just beginning their journey of self-realisation. All these individuals are born at precise times in order to be part of a coherent pattern of Evolution. Saturn, whose cycle is about twenty-nine years, marks out the limits of each generation. This is seen in that most families have usually a twenty- to thirty-year gap between parents and children.

Saturn is the principle of understanding in Kabbalah. By the time of the Saturn Return, at about twenty-nine years of age, many people have established the basis of their life. Any youthful illusions have usually been tempered by experiencing success, failure and the responsibility of a family. Also by this time parents have begun to age and the grandparent generation has started to die off. This stimulates reflection about life, death and what understanding there is of them, according to one's level of development. This is the hallmark of the Saturn cycle.

The Uranus cycle is about eighty-four years or a full lifetime. This planetary principle, in Kabbalah, is concerned with wisdom or flashes of revelation about the significance of life. Old people often do not die until such an insight occurs and then they discarnate soon after. About mid-way through the Uranus cycle, at around forty, comes what is commonly known as the 'mid-life crisis'. This is due to Uranus coming into opposition to its original natal position in an individual's birth chart. It is a period of disruption and confusion, out of which can come a new direction or a correction of a negative lifestyle. If the opportunity of a Uranian reorientation is not taken up, individuals often begin to slow down as their physical vitality, which peaks at this point, starts to weaken. The effect on the mind that does not seek to

90

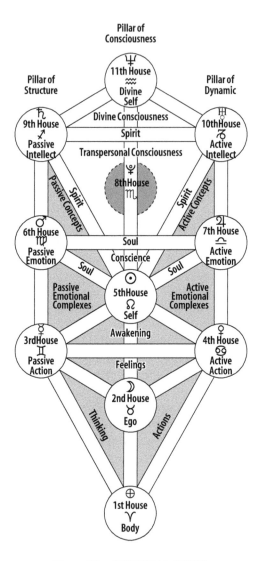

Figure 28—SPIRITUAL LEVEL
The four outer planets of Saturn, Uranus, Neptune and Pluto make up what is
called the Upper Face of the Tree. They represent the deep intellectual and
spiritual aspects of the psyche. Saturn and Uranus can be seen as Reason and
Revelation while Neptune represents the psyche's contact with the Divine where the
three upper Worlds meet. Pluto, which is half in and half out of the Solar system,
is the mystical component of the mind. These planets are only directly active in
those who have developed to a high degree. Most people, during their transits,
might think about the meaning of life but not do anything about it. (Halevi.)

develop is that it becomes increasingly rigid, staid and arid. In most people this results in a crystallisation that can lead to psychological death long before the body ceases to function.

For those who open up to a wider field during their Uranus opposition, the perception of life alters greatly. They begin to see how their years of experience indicate the direction of their destiny. Here is where Pluto, the principle of transformation, begins to have a direct influence, in that the individual begins to recognise that fate is a culmination of karma. For those who are well advanced in this viewpoint, death is but a junction in a long sequence of lives in which this incarnation expresses the state of their situation. This perception enables a person to live on with the knowledge that they are part of a vast process and, if ready, a member of a particular soul group with a specific purpose.

Neptune defines, as said, the Divine dimension of each generation. As the planet passes through the Zodiac, so that soul group worships what the sign represents. This remote planet has a 164-year cycle, which can be seen in the epochs of history. Many Egyptian dynasties lasted about this length of time, as did the Golden Age of Greece and medieval scholasticism. Pluto has an orbit of 248 years, which marks the cycle of destruction and regeneration in history. The Reformation, which broke the absolute power of the Catholic Church, and the Renaissance, which brought the modern world into being, are examples. Pluto was in its own sign, Scorpio, when the degenerate Rodrigo Borgia became Pope Alexander VI and Columbus discovered the New World in 1492. These two events marked the end and beginning of eras.

The outer planets have a distinct influence on world affairs. This can be seen very precisely in the early 19th century when Saturn was moving though Leo triggering the imperialistic adventures of Napoleon. He had Sun in Leo with Moon in Capricorn. Having transformed the French Revolution into a personal domain, Napoleon extended his rule over much of Europe. This was possible because Uranus was passing through Libra at the time which tends to upset the balance of power. Taking advantage of such a situation, Napoleon assaulted his enemies with the idea of popular freedom as well as his armies. This undermined the old feudal order that had held Christendom together for centuries. Neptune in Scorpio turned many people at that time against religion, in a violent anti-cleric movement while Pluto was in Pisces and square to Sagittarius, the traditional signs of religion. This combination undermined papal authority.

Napoleon annexed the Vatican's territories and called his son King of Rome.

Between 1810 and 1820, as Uranus and Neptune moved through Sagittarius, an epoch of hope emerged after the defeat of Napoleon. This manifested in the Romantic movement that moved away from the precise forms of the 18th century arts into a more amorphous and radical mode. The flamboyant poetry of people like Byron was distinctly Sagittarian in its style while Pluto in Pisces expressed itself in Mary Shelley's disturbing novel *Frankenstein*. In contrast to the now outmoded discipline of Mozart, musicians such as Chopin and Beethoven composed a wide span of mood music while painters such as Turner and Daumier produced dramatic images of Nature and ordinary people. Meanwhile, writers like Dickens and Zola rejected the heroic novel and wrote realistic books about everyday life.

In 1848, when Neptune entered Pisces (vision), Uranus and Pluto were in Aries (war), square to Jupiter (power) and Mercury (students) in Cancer (community). This precipitated a series of revolutions in France, Austria, Germany, Italy, Hungary and Poland when the middle classes, led by students, challenged their governments. However, such idealistic reforms were thwarted by the violent reaction of every Establishment. All the rebellions were quickly put down by Mars in Leo, the military under royal authority. Saturn in Pisces gave rise to disillusion, defeatism and depression, causing many Europeans to migrate to the Americas. However, in the 1860s Uranus was in Gemini, causing a crisis as it conjoined the United States' natal Mars and Ascendant which resulted in the Civil War. At the same time another civil war went on in Italy. German-speaking troops of Prussia and Austria fought each other and there was a revolt in China.

Of course such events are not just due to the movements of the planets but the loading of a country's karma. This is not unlike an avalanche which only needs a sharp sound or change in temperature to start a slide. This can be seen in the build up to the First World War in which the major powers of Europe, struggling over who would dominate the world, met their nemesis in the biggest conflict since the Napoleonic epoch. For five centuries Europe had exploited less advanced peoples of the world and abused its privileged position. The first Great War destroyed the West's claim to be the most civilised of cultures by its sheer savagery. When it began in August 1914, Pluto had just entered the sign of Cancer, indicating mass death in this continental family.

Figure 29—GENERATION
Between 1891 and 1898, Uranus was in Scorpio while Neptune and Pluto were
transiting Gemini. Those born around this time were to be part of a generation
that was to fight in the Great European civil war of 1914 to 1918. Some ten
million were to die in the competition between various Western empires. Uranus
in Scorpio indicated a deadly reckoning while Neptune and Pluto created confusion
and fraternal killing. All marched off to war believing that God was on their side.
The reason for such a nemesis was both collective and individual negative karma
for the West's exploitation of the rest of the world. (Troops on the Western Front,
etching of World War I.)

Needless to say, the millions who had been killed in that terrible conflict were resentful at having had their lives cut short. Many were reborn immediately after 1918 in the baby boom that generally follows mass disasters as Nature seeks to re-establish a population. Not a few of these souls regarded the First World War as unfinished business and so by the 1930s, as the new generation reached military age, they were eager for action, along with those who had survived the trenches. This was especially true in Germany, a Scorpionic country, where many wanted revenge because of their defeat and to reinstate the nation as a great power.

All that was needed was a leader. He came in the form of Adolf Hitler. We shall examine his chart in detail later. As Saturn entered Aries in 1937, a rearmed Nazi Germany openly prepared for war. Conflict broke out as Pluto entered Leo in 1939 when Germany invaded Poland. This forced France and Britain to fight as both recognised the German threat to dominate Europe. In 1940 these Allies suffered several military setbacks as Pluto ploughed through Leo, France's Sun sign, while Mars afflicted England's Pisces Moon. Germany, however, had its brief hour of military glory but at a terrible cost in life as Pluto squared Scorpio. Hitler had said 'If there has to be blood spilt, let it be now'. And so it was, as his megalomania became the mad bull of his Taurean nature and the shadow side of Germany's Scorpionic temperament. The result was the destruction of a once great nation and the suicide of Hitler.

How, one may ask, is it possible for the Sun, Moon and planets to influence whole populations? The answer is, as said, that every human being is modelled on the same set of principles. Let us look at our example, Peter, to see how one individual, like millions of others, can resonate to the celestial input because of the subtle complexity of the instrument of the mind.

14. Resonance

The psyche is a delicate instrument with many strings. These may be seen in the twenty-two paths between the sefirot or celestial principles. As such they resonate from either end or in triads generating a wide variety of psychological activity. These paths are tuned by the particular signs which the Sun, Moon and planets occupy. Moreover, the tension of each string or path is affected by the flows of a celestial impulse from one end or the other during a transit. These are the subtle antennae of the psyche.

Thus if Mars, in a Tree-chart, is activated by a conjunction or trine, for instance, the flow of frequency going out from the sefirah of Judgement will move down the four paths connected with it to influence whatever is at the other end, in this case Mercury, Jupiter, Saturn and the Sun. With a Lunar transit, the resonance would be out to the inferior planets, the Ascendant and Sun. This in turn would affect the triads of thought, feeling and action as well as the triangle of Awakening.

The implication of this is that the whole of the psyche is vibrating and flowing like an Aeolian harp. These ancient instruments were hung up in the wind and made melodious sounds according to how they were tuned. The same principle applies here, since the psyche is set at the moment of birth to respond to a particular combination of celestial notes. The same arrangement is to be found, as noted, in radio and TV receivers which are designed to pick up certain frequencies and turn them into intelligible sound and images sent from afar. There is, in fact, no mystery as to how the celestial bodies influence us. As modern science has discovered, the heavens are full of emanating sources of radiation that are part of the known and unknown electromagnetic spectrum.

Of particular interest to the kabbalistic astrologer is how, exactly, they affect a particular psyche. The most obvious phenomenon is the power of the Sun and Moon over the mind and body. They clearly influence mental moods and physical vitality from day to day. Less observable is the fact that when Mars conjoins Mercury, people tend

96

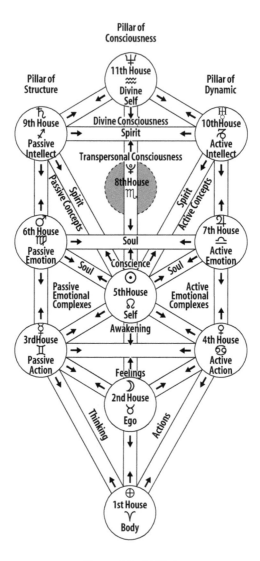

Figure 30—PATHS
Here the influences along the paths between the sefirot have to be taken into account. For example, the soul triad has a sextile between the Sun in Leo and Jupiter in Libra in the 5th and 7th Houses while there is no strong connection between the two emotional planets, Mars and Jupiter. This suggests that the expansive factor of the Self and charity embodied in Jupiter would offset the excessive critical element of Mars. This would give the soul a more balanced conscience. This is possible with a person who is aware of the workings of their psyche and is prepared to change an inherent pattern. (Halevi.)

to become fastidious as the path between them in the Tree of the psyche is activated. The same is true of any transit that stimulates the other twenty-one paths, either in the collective psyche or in an individual horoscope. In the former case it might manifest in a dull day in the stock market and in the latter a very particular state that can range from mania, through being alert, to a quiet peace or even as far as deep depression.

Because of free will, an individual can decide to go with such trends or oppose the impulse, reverse the flow along a path and so alter the character of the moment or their psychological activity. An example would be to counteract a mood of despondency coming down from an afflicted Saturn by applying Martial discipline up that path which joins them. This would contain a black mood and hold the mind steady until the negative transit has passed.

In the case of Peter, his Mercury in Gemini and his Venus in Cancer together with his Aries Ascendant would make him have a stop-go gut reaction in certain situations as the Moon circled the Zodiac each month. These responses would affect his thinking, feeling and action triads, as well as the ego, to produce a confused comprehension of what was going on from time to time. For instance, at work he might find that on some days he is very sharp and on others fuzzy in thought, feeling and action. At the same time, with a Sun transit, his awakening triad of Mercury-Sun-Venus might make him suddenly see the way he was behaving. This could alter the perception of his behaviour as all the paths of the lower mind were illuminated by an important Solar insight. Whether this observation was acted upon would depend on a decision to develop or not. If he were just living off his Moon, nothing would happen as the incident would soon be forgotten. In contrast, should he be working from the self of the Sun, then he could break the pattern of an ego habit.

As music can make one relax or want to dance, so the celestial melodies have a similar effect on the mind. In some cases a particular astrological transit will stimulate old memories. For example, when Jupiter traverses the 7th House of a birth chart every twelve years or so, the active emotional complexes that reside in that Sun-Jupiter-Venus triad will be aroused. Memories of relationships will arise, especially those of around twelve years and twenty-four years before. Of course, these might generate regret as well as comfort as nothing in the psyche is isolated, even in the unconscious.

This is because everything else is connected via all the paths of the

Tree, so a transit would reverberate throughout the mind like a shivering spider's web. Because Venus is directly connected to Jupiter, Peter might recall an incident in his youth of making love on a summer's night in a field. But then he would also remember how the girl eventually rejected him because he was not ready, if ever, for a permanent commitment. This would stimulate the left-hand emotional triad of Mars, Mercury and the Sun into action, to bring pain, disappointment and perhaps anger into consciousness.

Here the soul triad of the Sun, Mars and Jupiter could be alerted to consider his contribution to the end of the affair. He might see that his behaviour did not inspire any deep confidence in the girl. Often such a conclusion is triggered by another transit going on. Perhaps Venus is squared both to the current and natal position of Jupiter, adding to the painful memory, while a Mars transit causes Peter to criticise his conduct. All these inner events and memories would set up a reverberating flow through the paths and triads of his Tree-chart, beginning a psychological process that, if he went with it, could bring about an important transformation in his attitude to women.

By observing and examining the astrological impact of various transits and their effect on the Tree of the psyche, it is possible to get to know how the unconscious of a particular person operates. This is very useful when dealing with both external and internal problems which are often interrelated. To know what is going on deep in the mind, and to see what fate is pointing out, can help to avoid much unnecessary suffering and indicate when and what to do in an important situation.

If Peter was interested in self-development, he might go to an astrologer to get a reading of his chart. This could be a detailed technical description, which he did not understand, or a vague psycho-babble outline of his problem which leaves him more confused than before. The art of explaining a birth chart is to perceive what the client wants, not to give a lecture based upon the astrologer's psychological projection. A good consultant is well aware that their personal opinion can colour an objective conclusion.

In order to learn how to be impartial, an astrologer needs to know their own horoscope well and take into account their own bias and problems. It is not easy, for instance, for an intellectual practitioner to grasp how an action person experiences life. Likewise a 'feeler' astrologer has to learn what it is like to think through a situation so that they can see what it is like for someone with, say, a strong Gemini. All these skills have to be cultivated.

This is done by getting to know the kabbalistic Tree-chart really well and applying it to one's own horoscope. The triads, for example, give great detail into the usually inaccessible areas of the psyche. Let us examine them in the light of their astrological and psychological significance.

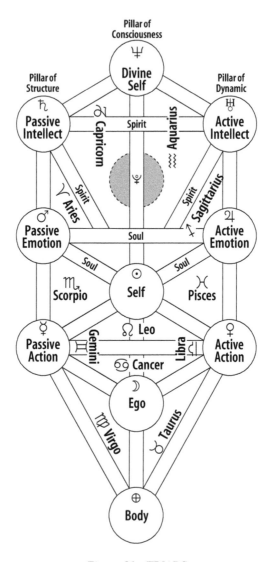

Figure 31—TRIADS

In this scheme, each triad is ruled by a specific sign because it is directly connected to the planet of a particular sefirah, such as Hod which governs Gemini and Virgo. Now if, for example, we have Mars in Gemini, that triad will be affected to make the person's intuition very sharp. This Mercury, Sun and Mars triad in the psyche is the one that can pick up the subtle reverberations given off by, say, envy. The Sun then perceives the source while Mars assesses the situation. The result may be evasive action or confrontation, according to the active or passive loading of the chart. (Halevi.)

15. Triads

Most of the triads on the Tree have a zodiacal sign (Figure 31). This relates to the nearest planet or luminary. Those triads without such a designation are the soul, spirit and Divine triangles as well as the large one composed of Mercury, Venus and the Ascendant. This is seen as the triad of vital soul. Especially to be noted are the horizontal triads of Leo and Cancer which are concerned with the Solar and Lunar levels of consciousness.

In our example, Peter has Mars in Virgo. This would affect the thinking triad, making it very exacting, while his Moon in Taurus would make the triad of action oscillate according to mood. Venus in the feeling triad, ruled by Cancer, would increase its already high level of volatility. In contrast, the Sun in its own sign, in the awakening triad, would heighten Peter's sense of his own importance.

The right-hand side triad of Libra, or desires and drives, has Jupiter in it. This expansive planet could cause the active introvert function to project its impulses outward. An example of this might be a compulsive movement such as twitching. Mercury in Gemini, in the side triad opposite and in its own sign, would intensify the introvert function of intuition. This could turn its normal receptivity into an active instrument to be directed consciously. For instance, Peter might use it to probe people's minds telepathically, if he knew he had this talent.

Pluto in the passive emotional triad might arouse some previous life fears as well as current ones while its opposite, the active emotional triad where the North Node is posited, could give Peter a certain emotional arrogance. Conversely the South Node in Virgo, with Mars there, might make him even more critical of himself as well as others. By taking such note of what is in each triad, a detailed picture can be built up of the qualities and quirks of the psyche's make up as well as its general disposition.

For example, in this chart Saturn is in the active intellectual triad of Sagittarius. This would have the effect of making Peter extremely firm in his belief system. If he had lived in the 11th century, he might have been a zealous Crusader or, during the French Revolution, an ardent republican. Being born in the 20th century and in the West, he could be politically radical or conservative but convinced that his view was the correct one.

Looking at the highest level of the Tree, Uranus in the Capricorn triad of transpersonal experience would precipitate, deep within Peter's unconscious, moments of profound understanding. In contrast, Neptune in his active transpersonal triad might open up an intellectual aspiration to enter the Divine dimension. This of course could only happen if he had done a great deal of interior work to bring the unconscious into consciousness. If he were still at the vegetable or animal level, he would be only dimly aware of what might be going on in the hidden depths of his mind.

The triads of the central column, that is the vital, soul, spiritual and Divine levels, represent different degrees of consciousness. While the lower part of the Tree-chart is governed by physical factors and psychological habits, the soul is not. This soul triad in particular is a very important component of the psyche, for it is not directly subject to the Worlds below or above it. Although influenced by the adjacent emotional and intellectual triads, it is not bound by them. Here is where free will is exercised when a person begins to live off their Sun and individuate. This is possible because the Sun-self is the pivot of the psychological system and can call upon Jupiter and Mars to expand or contract emotionally, to open or close the intellect or to make an important decision. In Shakespeare's Julius Caesar, Cassius says, 'The fault, dear Brutus, is not in our stars, but in ourselves, that we are underlings'. Shakespeare understood the soul's relation to the rest of the psyche, which is why he was a great playwright.

While choice is possible at the level of the soul, it is not in the great triad of the spirit composed of the Sun, Saturn and Uranus. This zone of the mind is beyond most people because it is cosmic in dimension. Only well-advanced individuals have access to this transpersonal realm. This is the place of mystical vision and the Heavenly Chambers spoken of by great sages, saints and prophets. It is at this psycho-spiritual frontier that an evolving individual gives up personal ambition and surrenders themselves to their destiny. If our Peter attained this level, he would know, by the positions of his planets, Moon and Sun, what his purpose in existence was. In his case, his full potential would indeed be to become a leader, because of his Sun in Leo in the 5th

Figure 32—DEATH
Julius Caesar had clear indications of his imminent death. The night before he was assassinated he was asked how he would like to die. His reply was, 'Suddenly'. His wife had a warning dream and suggested he should stay at home that day and a note was sent to him, telling of danger. He ignored all the omens and was murdered. This incident indicates that the moment of death is not absolutely preordained. Caesar could have avoided it. An astrologer of a later period saw certain death in his own chart but it turned out that it was a way of living that came to an end, not his life. Pluto, the planet of death, is also that of rebirth. It all depends upon the level involved. Evolved individuals are not subject to general laws. (Caesar's Death, 17th century engraving).

House. As such, he would radiate a certain charisma by his very being. This is indicated by Saturn in Sagittarius in the 9th House and Uranus in Capricorn in the 10th House. Pluto in its own sign in the 8th House would suggest that he might have been an advanced individual over many lives—if he had attained enlightenment at some point in the past. Needless to say, he would be a rare kind of person. The present Dalai Lama has this quality.

Illumination is the concern of the Divine triad of Saturn, Uranus and Neptune. Their positions and relationship reveal what Divinity would mean to Peter if he had, or were to, attain such a state. If he did, his Sun in Leo would attract many people to him. If he were not in a high official position, then he might be an influential advisor to those in power. Plotinus, the great Neo-Platonic teacher, was on personal terms with a Roman emperor although he held no formal court position.

Such remarkable individuals change the course of history. Some may well be Pisceans whose presence in government is not conspicuous. Others might be captains of industry, great merchants or even in the military. There have been many evolved souls who have been close to the seat of government, much to the annoyance of ambitious, animal level people.

There is a legend of how a jealous minister took the king's wise astrologer up a tower with the intention of pushing him off. The courtier, out of sadistic pleasure, asked the sage if he knew the day of his death. The astrologer, well aware of the situation, replied that it was interesting to note astrologically that the minister would be killed the day after he died. From that time on the astrologer came under the courtier's personal protection.

There can be little doubt that the astrologer periodically consulted his own chart and knew that a critical transit was coming up. But being conscious of such celestial events is not enough. He had to be acutely alert to what was going on in the world around him, unlike the strolling astrologer who fell down a hole one night while looking up at the sky.

16. Transits

Now while the Solar, Lunar and planetary principles are crystallised in a birth chart, the actual celestial bodies move on. Moreover, they do not progress in a random pattern. While the Earth turns in a day and takes around 365 days to circle the Sun, the Moon has, besides its 28-day orbit, an 18-year sub-cycle. Mercury and Venus go round the Sun in less than a year while Mars takes two years, Jupiter twelve, Saturn twenty-nine, Uranus about eighty-four, Neptune one hundred and sixty-four and Pluto two hundred and forty-eight. This means that each takes a certain time to move through one zodiacal sign. In the case of the inferior planets, between Earth and the Sun, it is a matter of weeks while Mars takes about two months, Jupiter a year, Saturn about two-and-a-half years and Uranus, Neptune and Pluto taking around seven, thirteen and twenty years respectively.

None of these zodiacal transits is of exact duration and some vary greatly. However, what has been observed is that they have a distinct effect on a horoscope, be it a personal or collective chart. Let us take, for example, that of the United States in 1973 when Saturn, the principle of constriction, entered Cancer, the Sun sign of the USA. At this point, as could be expected, the Vietnam War in which it was engaged took a downturn. Despite its overwhelming military power, America was losing the battle against a small people who had been trying to free themselves of French colonial rule and now American domination. While thousands of Vietnamese were being killed, so too were many Americans under the most horrible jungle conditions. This went on until Saturn left Cancer, the sign of the mass of people.

Meanwhile, Americans at home were depressed, not only about their first impending military defeat but also about the scandal going on in Washington. The then President, Richard Nixon, a Capricorn, had Saturn opposing his Sun. This brought out his shadow side, the manipulative aspect of Cancer, which manifested in the exposure of secret recordings and the burglary of his political opponents' offices. America, then in economic recession as Saturn conjoined Mercury,

Venus and Jupiter, as well as the Sun, in America's 2nd House of wealth, went into shock. Mars passing through Cancer added outrage at the revelations which caused many people to demonstrate against the government and the President in particular.

For Nixon it was an extremely personal matter, as his Sun in the 5th House of leadership was battered by the opposition of Saturn and the other planets in Cancer. His sinking reputation was made worse as his Aquarius Moon was opposed by Saturn moving on into Leo in the summer of 1974. In the June of that year, his body started to react to all this pressure. He became ill with phlebitis, an inflammation of a vein in the lower leg. This limb is ruled by Aquarius while Leo (ruler of the heart) governs circulation. Besides his deteriorating health, Nixon was forced to consider his political position, as he was likely to be impeached for abusing power. This was a bitter decision for a very ambitious Capricorn at the crest of worldly achievement. The breaking point occurred just when the Sun came into full opposition to his natal Moon on the eighth of August 1974 and the Moon in Aries squared his and America's natal Suns. On that day Nixon became the first American President to resign.

This example illustrates how two entities, a nation and a person, can be involved in the same event because there are correspondences that link their fates. It is interesting to note, in another example, that Captain Smith of the Titanic had Neptune (delusion and water) in his 8th House, denoting death by drowning due to the mistaken belief that his ship was unsinkable. When the Titanic was launched on May 31st 1911, Mars was in the Watery sign of Pisces and squared to Pluto, the principle of Nemesis, in Gemini, the Airy sign of speedy travel. Had the liner not been sailing so swiftly, the iceberg might have been seen in time and the ship, the epitome of the latest technology, would not have sunk with the loss of some 1,500 lives. Another view is that, perhaps, all who were drowned were destined, because of karma, to die in that way. This is a factor to consider in any collective event. The converse evidence is that some people do not get killed in even worse accidents.

Are such events inevitable? This is an important question. As noted earlier, while the overall plan of existence is fixed, the fates of individuals and nations can vary within their context. This means that a conscious or wise decision can avert a crisis and extend the life of an individual. The day of death is not absolutely fixed in a chart but can occur with certain transits. Most people, being creatures of habit,

Figure 33—KARMA
This picture is in a series about a good and a bad apprentice. They begin as equals but, over time, their lives unfold in different ways according to their conduct. The good one becomes a master of his profession, while the other turns into a criminal. In this scene, one—the good, now a magistrate—has to send his old colleague to the gallows. The series depicts stages of choice and their result. The same is true of a birth chart. One can exploit or abuse it. Every horoscope has its easy and difficult aspects. What we do with them is our responsibility.
(Hogarth's *The Industrious Prentice Alderman of London,* 18th century.)

will die at a predictable point, for example if they drink or smoke heavily or live a stressful life. On the collective level, nations will also inevitably court disaster, like the Japanese militaristic government of the 1930s and 40s. To attack the American naval base of Pearl Harbor was to go to war with the most powerful country in the world. Moreover, their brutal bombing and massacres of the Chinese were bound to generate a terrible karma which manifested in the near total destruction of their homeland. This need not have happened if the Japanese people had not agreed to serve the emperor without thought.

At the individual level, transits can stimulate certain frames of mind. This is seen in psychopaths who can swing between mania and depression as their Tree-chart is rocked, perhaps by a powerful opposition or square from Uranus or Saturn. A severely afflicted natal Mars can produce a psychological tension which will produce a certain chemical reaction in the body. Most physicians believe that a metabolic imbalance is the cause of such psychotic episodes and not that they are the result of something more subtle. The 17th century book *The Anatomy of Melancholy* is full of astrological data about what configurations unbalance the mind but few modern psychiatrists take this into account.

When the mind is under great stress due to outer circumstance and pressing celestial conditions, latent psychopathic tendencies can manifest. For instance, President Nixon had his natal Mars in Sagittarius which made him unusually impulsive for a Capricorn. He also had Mercury conjunct Mars in his chart which made him potentially paranoid. His deteriorating personal and political position brought out this fatal flaw, enhanced by Saturn in Cancer opposing his Sun. An evolved individual could have transformed this tension and become the great captain guiding the nation through an historic storm.

Unfortunately Nixon, nicknamed 'Tricky Dicky', was not of this calibre. He was a corrupted animal man who had made his name by being a member of the inquisitorial Committee of Un-American Activities in the 1950s. This was a witch-hunting team seeking out Communists, headed by the tyrannical Senator McCarthy who was a nasty Scorpio. The Committee's methods induced fear into American culture. People's careers and reputations were ruined by McCarthy's ruthless interrogation, backed by Nixon. Any evidence or hint of association with Communism was exploited, even if just hearsay. Nixon paid for this early period in his life as karma caught up with him. The result was that he became so paranoid that he was prepared to send members of his presidential team to burgle his political rival's office.

The lesson here is to be aware of what transits are going on or are imminent so that one may be prepared to weather a storm, accept a calm or exploit a dynamic celestial and terrestrial situation. This brings us to progressions, yet another dimension to the Divine plan.

17. Progressions

The laws of Existence work at many levels. In the body there are a number of rhythms, some short, some long and some in-between. These are carefully co-ordinated by an overall plan which adjusts to different circumstances such as time of day, season and physical age. It is very clear to anyone suffering from jet-lag that these cycles are carefully rematched. In astrology there are planetary rhythms that relate to the birth chart such as the Jupiterian cycle and Saturn return. However, there are other, more subtle, astrological processes called progressions.

One of these is the motion of the Sun from its original natal position, symbolised by one degree for each year of a life. The effect is not unlike a deep current that indirectly influences the surface of the sea of fate. During a lifetime the progressed Sun may traverse several zodiacal signs and houses. Thus if someone is born with Sun in Cancer in the 12th House, but near the Ascendant, they may experience a period of being drawn out and exposed as their progressed Sun passes into Leo and the 1st House. This could manifest in a quiet, shy and insecure child becoming the much admired bright boy or gifted girl at school. As the Sun progression moves on, they may not live up to their golden image and indeed revert to being a Cancerian introvert again. Such a process could have a fatal impact.

In the example depicted in Figure 34, the subject has a Capricorn Sun in the 12th House. This would make Carol, as we will call her, a reflective, hard working introvert. The Moon in Aquarius in the 2nd House would incline her to be more interested in possessing power than wealth or comfort. She would be a manipulative innovator operating quietly within any organisation, whatever her status. Her ascending Lunar Node is in Taurus in the 4th House of security, along with Uranus. They would reinforce her political skill in achieving her long-term aim. Such an objective would be enhanced by Saturn in Gemini in the 6th House. Thus it would not be surprising that, after some years, she might be the personal assistant to the boss and be, in effect, the power behind the throne.

Her personal life would not be quite so well handled with Mars in Leo in the 7th House. This indicates that she would seek a successful and glamorous man for a marriage or business partner; indeed, she might also be the boss's mistress. However, with Pluto in Cancer in the same house there could be, despite any strong connection between them, many quarrels. This would rise in a crescendo as her progressed Sun conjoined her natal Moon. The issue would be over who was really the dominant partner. In this case, unless she lived off her more diplomatic Sun, her Fixed and obstinate Moon might destroy years of preparation, for example to take over a business. A disharmonious transit of her Uranus and Moon, not wisely handled, might push her abruptly out of the company onto the street in her forties. This would be a hard lesson.

As such a situation comes about partly because of her progressed Sun, so a similar effect would occur with the Lunar and planetary progressions that act as other deep currents of her fate. Let us look at Carol's early life in greater detail to get a sense of how these undertows function.

The first five years of her life, while the Sun was still in the 12th House, would suggest a very protected infancy. However, when the Sun crossed the Ascendant and entered the 1st House, Carol would come out of the confinement of her parental home and begin to play a part in the politics of her school playground. She would not be an academically bright pupil, because Capricorns are slow learners. However, in her early twenties she would begin to be quite astute, on account of the progressed Sun approaching her natal Mercury in Aquarius. She would become known for her unusual wit and her ability to spot problems and suggest solutions in any organisation with which she was involved. This would create a reputation she would build on.

As a 12th House Capricorn, she would observe the dynamics of her workplace and target useful people. She might, because of her Venus in Sagittarius in the 12th House, have a few discreet affairs to further her professional prospects. However, when her progressed Sun opposed her Mars in Leo, in the House of Partners, she might decide to exert pressure on an important lover to marry her, even though he already had a wife. Carol would be a kind of modern Lady Macbeth with ultimately the same disastrous result.

However, if she were living off her Sun rather than her Moon, her innate Capricornian sense of justice would begin to arouse her conscience. As usually happens, there would be a set of planetary

112

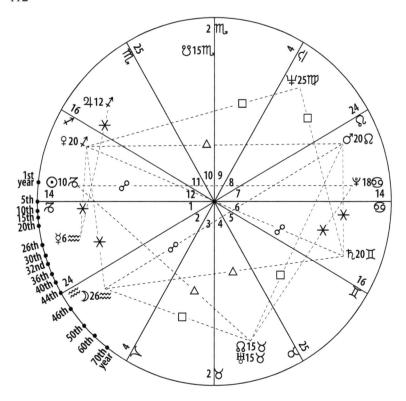

Figure 34—PROGRESSIONS
In a progression such as this, in which the Sun is moved a degree each year away
from its original position, a sub-plot can be observed. Around the fifth year, in
our example, when the Sun moves from the 12th House across the Ascendant and
into the 1st House, the child might find its outer circumstance radically changed.
Likewise, about the age of forty-four, another upheaval could occur. This,
however, would be influenced by the then positions of the celestial bodies at the
time. The significance of the progressions is that there are more levels in a life
than current transits. (Halevi.)

transits that would coincide with the progressed situation so as to bring about a decisive crisis. Carol would have to choose between her animal level compulsion and becoming a real human being. It would be a very soul-searching period, in which she would have to make up her mind before the opportunity, created by circumstance and celestial conditions, disappeared and the opportunity to further her ambition or inner development passed.

The painter, Gauguin, faced this problem and gave up solid, middle-class security to become a wandering bohemian when he was confronted by his Uranus opposition. However, the preparation for such a transition had been made by his progressed Sun which conjoined his natal Jupiter in Cancer in the 11th House. This could have made him very successful in business but when, in his forties, the progressed Sun conjoined his Mars in Leo and entered the 12th House, he decided he wanted to be an artist. He left his wife and five children and devoted himself to free love and painting. When he eventually migrated to the tropical isle of Tahiti, he set up a harem of native women and produced his finest work before dying far from home and any European culture. At the time of his death his progressed Sun was in his 12th house, the place of isolation.

The function of such progressions appears to be like an unconscious background to an individual's fate. A parallel is seen in the construction of a novel that has an overall story in which each character lives out a subplot. An example of this is Tolstoy's great work, *War and Peace*. In this, the vast panorama of the Napoleonic period is the setting for the hero's search for himself and the heroine's lesson about love. Both are caught up in an historic process to which even Napoleon is subject. Despite his military genius he could not defeat the Russian winter and so, inevitably, had to retreat. Even this man of destiny had to conform to a larger scheme.

To take the parallel further, Napoleon's brief period of power occurred because Europe had reached a particular stage of development. He filled a gap between the old feudal world and the modern state. This was part of the transition from the Piscean Age to that of Aquarius. He was the last of the absolute monarchs before political reform came in during the 19th century. Seen on a yet more vast scale, prior to that of Pisces came the Age of Aries. This epoch of the pioneer and warrior saw a period of exploration, invention and organised warfare. Before this came the Age of Taurus, the Earthy sign of the Bull, between roughly 5,000 and 3,000BCE when, as one might expect, humanity began by settling and farming to take over the possession of land from Nature.

According to this view, all and everything are part of cycles inside cycles and within cycles. This means there are limits to what is possible as nothing can operate outside its time and space, except human beings. Only they can descend to the depths and heights of Existence by conscious effort. While this gives individuals the power to explore the material realm and go beyond the angelics, it also means that, if they abuse their capability, then disease will occur.

18. Disease

18. Disease

Disease, as the word implies, means 'un-ease'. It applies when the body or the mind is unbalanced in any way to a degree where malfunction occurs. This is different from the normal processes of ageing and decay. In Nature there are times of excess, such as flood and drought, that cause death on a large scale but these events are usually corrected as the universe always seeks to balance and compensate a situation. However, in the case of humanity, free will, stupidity, thoughtlessness and many vices can generate illnesses that relate to a particular individual or community. Let us begin by examining the body, where disease is most easily recognised.

The human body is greatly influenced by what goes on in the mind. Culture, for example, can determine diet which, if deficient, can cause disease. Likewise unhealthy habits, such as drugs, can lead to a shortening of life. Whatever the reason, a birth chart can indicate where illness is likely to arise.

There are three basic kinds of disease. The transient inconvenience, such as influenza, the chronic malady, like a bad back, and the fatal illness. The flu is due to seasonal circumstance but it can be an expression of a general syndrome, like the great flu epidemic after the First World War when Saturn in Leo was opposed to Uranus in Aquarius, thus lowering the vitality level of millions already exhausted by conflicts and deprivation. A permanent backache may have its origin, like not be able to 'stomach' something, in a psychological problem; but here resulting from an afflicted Saturn, which rules the bones, or Moon which governs the stomach. Grave diseases are of a deeper order related to karma. These can have their source in a negative Sun configuration with Mars and Jupiter indicating a sickness of the soul.

In a birth chart, the potential site of illness in the body may be seen in certain astrological aspects. A Uranus square to the Ascendant might make someone accident prone while an affliction of Saturn or Capricorn could reveal a tendency towards skin maladies. This suggests that celestial transits, which stress the psyche, can resonate in the

116

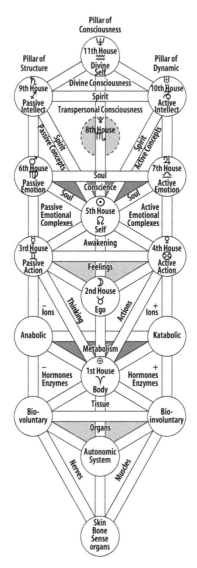

Figure 35—DISEASE

The physical and psychological Trees interconnect. They also resonate with the organs in the body. Thus, a broken heart can manifest as literal heartache. Likewise, a soul triad that is overloaded with fear will affect the metabolic triad below, causing adrenaline constantly to suffuse the body. These conditions can be created by the astrological set up of a birth chart or a strong or weak transit. Thus Saturn afflicting Venus could result in a chronic lack of energy for as long as the transit was in operation. (Halevi.)

body Tree to produce anything from not feeling well for a while to a deadly illness. An over-confident attitude, created by Mars in Aries which rules the head, can manifest as injuries to or pains in the skull, while a heavily afflicted Sun in Leo might lead to heart trouble. This could be due to long-term frustration or lack of recognition leading to coronary problems.

Take for example a man with Sun, Mercury and Venus in Virgo in the 6th House. Such a person would be preoccupied, if not obsessed with their health, giving rise to some nervous disorder that would erupt in a fever when an afflicted Mars squared the Sun or either of these inferior planets. The mechanism of the disorder is that the body may resonate violently to the Martial input that is agitating the mind. If the person denies what is going on in the psyche, then the pain will be referred to the body level in order to obtain release or draw attention to some psychological issue triggered by the Mars transit.

Another source of illness can come from an excessive loss of emotional and vital energy due to a trine between Jupiter and Venus. This natal configuration might cause a woman to take too many lovers or overeat. The result would be, in the body, for its activity to be overloaded on the right pillar, thus bringing about physical exhaustion. Harmonious aspects are not always favourable, as many believe. Indeed, any excess of trines or sextiles in a horoscope indicates a tendency towards a fatal psychological or physical weakness. The classic case of this is the person born into great wealth or privilege who has no 'spine' when under pressure.

Chronic anxiety, which is centred in the negative emotional complexes of the Tree, may be due to a heavy Saturn or Mars aspect. This can resonate with the metabolic triad of the physical Tree to such an extent that the body slowly becomes increasingly rigid. Such a stress could cause arthritis. The astrological loading of the Tree-chart is crucial as it indicates where illness might be latent. Being integrated systems, the physical and psychological Trees operate as one in life. This concept is accepted by some psychoanalysts and physicians but it is perceived as the norm in most esoteric traditions.

Diseases are the result of a deep and long discrepancy in the mind. Those who are not true to themselves, or live a life quite contrary to their fate, often develop a disorder of the soul that will result in some serious illness. An unacknowledged bad marriage, bitter resentment or hate can, over a long time, generate a referred sickness in the finer levels of the body. Such diseases are sometimes the legacy of an unresolved soul condition in a previous life. This may be the case in some of those who, ill from birth, develop certain degenerative diseases or die young from some fatal malady. An afflicted Pluto in the signs of Virgo and Scorpio, or the 6th and 8th Houses, can indicate a karmic carryover that needs attention if a disease-troubled life is to be avoided. Sometimes this is part of an individual's fate and a hard lesson has to be endured.

Purely mental illness is often due to an imbalance of planets on the psychological Tree. A manic-depressive might have a chart that is heavily afflicted on the left pillar, or *vice versa* with Uranus, Jupiter and Venus exerting excessive pressure. This can cause the Tree to swing to and fro to compensate. In some cases, a lack of connection between the Sun-self and the ego-Moon can engender a psychological conflict of reality versus fantasy as the mind tries to find a centre of gravity. While most people experience periodic anxiety, when celestial transits disturb their lives, those with an unbalanced chart can develop neurotic or even psychotic symptoms. Mussolini, the Italian dictator, had Moon conjunct Saturn, Mars and Pluto in Gemini, sextile the Sun in Leo in the 9th House. He could not have been anything else but a megalomaniac, especially with Uranus in the 10th House. Signs of his psychosis made themselves apparent quite early on when he stabbed his sweetheart and a friend. While his schizoid behaviour might be put down to having a devout Catholic mother and a fervent Communist father, the Gemini Moon, Mars, Saturn and Pluto were the cause of the fatal split in his mind.

Sickness of the soul can be, as noted, the result of good or bad aspects between Mars, Jupiter and the Sun that make up the triad. A person with such a planetary and Solar affliction may believe that fate has given them too hard a deal. Conversely with a grand trine, another individual may be unable to understand that life owes them nothing. Both might well see themselves as incapable of coping with life if they choose not to exploit their karmic situation. Someone perhaps experiencing a Uranus or Pluto transit might decide to commit suicide either suddenly or gradually by the whisky bottle. Sometimes the attempt is a ploy to get attention but this may not succeed and they die sooner or later when a death transit hits their chart. A case of this was a very beautiful, rich and aristocratic young woman who pushed her life into an area of destruction. She was killed with her lover in a car crash when Pluto squared her natal Pluto in the 8th House of Death. They need not have died if she had realised in time the foolish risk she was taking.

119

Figure 36—MEDICINE
In ancient and medieval times many physicians were also astrologers. They rec-
ognised that the body, as with the seasons, was affected by what was going on in
the heavens. So accordingly they chose the best time to administer a remedy.
These were also based upon cosmic resonance, in that certain plants and minerals
appeared to relate to a particular astrological principle. Some modern surgeons
have discovered that it is best to operate when the Moon is in a certain phase, as
it appears to be a factor in the body's ability to cope. (Woodcut, 16th century.)

Criminals are often psychotics. Take Al Capone, the American gangster boss. He had Sun in Capricorn and Mars in Cancer, square to Moon in Aries. Square to his Pisces Ascendant were Venus, Saturn and Pluto. Such a combination made him ambitious, aggressive and shrewd. By the age of thirty his cunning and cruelty made him master of the city of Chicago's gangsters and many others, including some congressional lawyers. He had the potential for high achievement, like his hero Napoleon, but his Tree-chart was distorted. With Neptune in Gemini deception, delusion and crime were his gods. Ironically, it was tax evasion that brought about his arrest. He died in jail from a syphiloid form of insanity, the Libra shadow side of his Aries Moon.

19. Choice

We have seen how life is a sequence of various ages. Each is a period of learning and choice that will affect those that follow. What happens can be the result of a series of seemingly insignificant moments or a single major turning point. Such events usually coincide with some transit peculiar to a specific birth chart or a general astrological situation. For example, the 1962 conjunction of Sun, Moon and five planets in Aquarius created a world crisis as India and China, the two most populous nations, confronted each other over a common border and Russia and America, the two most powerful, nearly went to war over rocket sites in Cuba. This massive conjunction of celestial bodies caused people to react in different ways, according to their culture and individual temperament. For example, many Hindus were zealous to fight for their homeland while others retreated into meditation. In Russia at least one general was quite ready to press the nuclear war button, while in England a young man who fancied a certain girl suggested they make love before the atomic missiles fell on London. Each individual has choice even in an international crisis.

Choice begins in the womb. As noted, a soul in the process of being born can perceive what its prospective parents are like. If a pregnancy is not wanted, the gestating infant body can be retarded by the soul's reluctance to enter into that couple's world. Out of such a decision can come a difficult fate. However, this may possibly be part of that individual's karma for they may have been a rejecting parent themselves in a previous existence. Such a possibility could be indicated in a Uranian configuration on the Ascendant or in the 8th House which might foreshadow chronic bad health or an early death. Even so, the faculty of free will could turn misfortune into an advantage as many disabled people have accomplished much. Stephen Hawking, the Capricornian astronomer who did important work on black holes in space and wrote the best-selling *A Brief History of Time*, suffers severely from motor neurone disease. He wanted to be a modern Isaac Newton and indeed was given his Chair at Cambridge University.

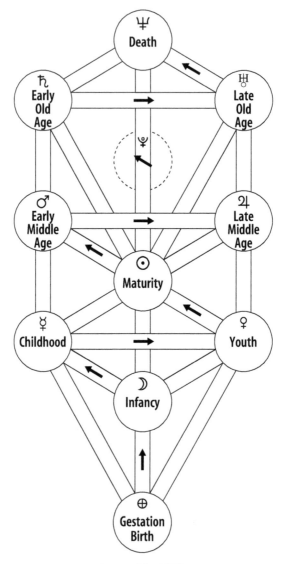

Figure 37—LIFE
These are the stages of incarnation. However, while a person may live all these out in the body, they may not mature beyond infancy or childhood psychologically. There are many middle-aged people who believe they are still eighteen. This can be due to a strong Venusian, Libran or Taurean factor in their birth chart or that they have 'fixated' at that youthful point of development. Many such men have this 'Casanova' syndrome and some women still play the 'femme fatale'. Those who seek to evolve move beyond the Sun. (Halevi.)

The next phase, that of the Moon when an infant orbits its mother, also contains moments of choice. The soul may choose to accept life as it is or be angry about its lot. One mother noted that in the forty years she had known her son, his fury at being born was still strongly with him. He fought everything and everybody until his old age and so, no doubt, he will repeat the same pattern over again in future fates, until he chooses to learn to change.

As is well known, the emotional investment of expectation of parents in a child is quite common. This leads to them projecting a whole set of hopes as the child begins to develop an ego. As the Moon mind is trained into family customs, so it develops a particular approach. This is partly determined by what sign the Moon is in. Thus the Watery quality of a Pisces Moon will combine with the acquired cultural attitudes. How this persona is used is up to the individual, who may be dominated by their situation or use it, like an actor does, as a conscious mask to cover what is really going on in the mind. This choice is quite crucial in the way one relates to others and the world.

The Mercurial phase of life, between the ages of seven and fourteen, develops the thinking triad of the psychological Tree. If Mercury is afflicted in a child's chart, then they have to choose to work hard at school or remain mentally untrained. In contrast, a child with a well aspected Mercury will be an excellent scholar but such cleverness can lead to a kind of laziness, because of over-confidence. Here again is choice. The same is true of the Venusian phase of adolescence. When puberty sets in, there will be the strong desire to explore sexuality. While a well-placed Venus will offer one kind of choice, an afflicted Venus will present another. In both cases a decision will have to be taken as regards how to handle passion; the nature of which will also depend upon Venus' astrological position. In some cases, a lack of aspects or many could be critical. The former might create a heartless femme fatale and the latter a Don Juan. The libertine, Casanova, had Mercury, Venus, Mars and Jupiter in Pisces with Sun in Aries. This Watery and Fiery combination generated an endless need to seduce women, all of whom he declared he loved, until he became bored or too involved. At some point Casanova must have chosen his lifestyle. In old age he ended up alone and unloved. Such is karma.

Taking on responsibility for one's life is one of the signs of Solar maturity. Upon becoming physically fully grown, people have to choose whether to be adult or not. Some take on the challenge but others are not prepared to accept that whatever happens is their own fault or to their credit. Such people choose to remain at the Mercurial and Venusian stages, playing games or acting like adolescents far beyond their youth. Not a few prefer to fantasise about what they want to be while living a life in which they have no great pleasure or prospects. This is perhaps one of the most important choices. It turns millions into followers of others who may be popular celebrities they admire, like elder brothers and sisters, or parental figures such as politicians who promise to look after them if they vote for their party.

One does not have to follow the crowd which is subject to the Lunar tidal law that governs mass movements. If one chooses to live off one's Sun, then wider possibilities open up. A man who runs a small shop in a village can at least be his own master, while a well paid executive in a large company may be no more than an easily replaceable servant. There are many well-heeled slaves to be found high in government, big business and grand homes, while men and women in control of their own lives are quite rare. Such people may be employees but they are not to be bought. They have a certain integrity because they have chosen not to be ruled by their Moon or Ascendant. They often stand out as the only adult around, to whom everyone else goes with their personal problems. Bosses and heads of departments hate them.

An excellent example of this kind of real individual were the American explorers, hunters and pioneers who opened up the Wild West. They were self-reliant, brave and ingenious. Joseph Walker, a 19th century trailblazer, for instance, was recognised both by whites and Indians as a natural aristocrat, even though he lived rough like them. He was the epitome of a leader who had attained not only a practical authority but an inner maturity. Seen on Jacob's Ladder, Walker had reached the top of the physical Tree and the central Solar pivot of the psychological Tree. Here also is to be found the bottom sefirah of the spiritual Tree which makes the third, transpersonal component of the self.

When these three Solar levels fuse, an individuated person becomes a man or woman of destiny. This leads to a decision as to whether to take on one's mission or not. Free will allows the choice to refuse. Some advanced people prefer a quiet life. Lao Tsu, the Chinese sage, chose this option when he took to the mountains to get away from an incurably corrupt imperial court. This illustrates how fate can be modified if one has conscious control.

The Martial period of life of one's thirties and forties is particularly

Figure 38—CHOICE
There are critical points in life when we have to make an important decision.
These usually occur when there is a powerful transit affecting our chart. The
issue is generally a lesser or greater option. The latter requires more effort and
risk, but has a better payoff, while in the former there is no commitment, it is
safer and not so exhausting. This, however, has no real reward. Such a choice
can be about a relationship, a job or some enterprise. Most choose the easier
option so as to be secure while the others, realising security is an illusion, take
on the gamble and choose the 'High Road'. (Tarot.)

concerned with choice. In the struggle to establish a position in life, constant decisions have to be made. Some are fatal. The wrong conclusion by a man can ruin a career while a bad action of a woman can destroy a child's trust. Such events are not uncommon and can leave a scar on someone's life. Conversely, a wise choice can alter a whole family's possibilities. Many who risked migrating to the Americas did not regret that fatal decision. It changed their situation from poverty to prosperity with yet other opportunities.

The Jupiterian epoch of middle age has fewer obvious choices but they are there. The issues may no longer be about worldly matters as they, by now, would usually have been settled one way or another. The question would be, what to do after retirement. When both occupation and children are gone, a new kind of life has to be lived. The choice is either to sink into decline or to develop further. Many die soon after retirement as they were too dependent on their work routine to support them. The world now no longer needs their skills which can soon become obsolete as progress passes them by, leaving them bereft of purpose, unless they choose to reflect on their life's lessons.

The Saturnian period is about such preoccupations. Looking back over life reveals how certain events fit into a distinct pattern. Mistakes made, obstinate attitudes or even evil inclinations might be unpleasant insights but, with the combination of the Solar and Saturnian aspects of the mind, much good may also be perceived. While it may be too late to correct what was not right, consideration and decisions as regards the hereafter or next life have to be taken into account, especially in the light of sudden Uranian revelations about one's fate, beginning to come in late old age.

The Plutonian principle of mystical knowledge, which can be experienced at any point of life, will now certainly come to the forefront of a dying person's consciousness. There may be flashes of the remote past and the distant future that relate to the present. When all these come together, the choice comes whether to die with ease or cling on to the decaying body. This is perhaps the most crucial of choices as it could determine what will happen after death and in the next life. At the moment of departure, people encounter the power of Neptune, the realm of the Divine. Here is where the final choice is made.

20. Crisis

One of the chief precipitators of choice is crisis. A crisis is when various factors come into apparent collision or when a contradiction has to be resolved. This can occur at any time or level. Whatever the issue, it involves a decision. As noted, the state of the cosmos usually has some influence on such a situation, be it a national crisis or a turning point of a person's fate.

During the mid-1930s a certain female soul was first conceived about the time Saturn was in Pisces, Uranus in Taurus, Neptune in Virgo and Pluto in Cancer. As the last three were retrograde, so a pause occurred in the cosmic process which allowed her to decide not to be incarnated at that point. A parallel in worldly affairs was the Western democracies' hesitancy to check Nazi Germany and Fascist Italy in their territorial expansions. By 1938 the clouds of war were gathering as Jupiter squared Neptune and Saturn, generating a vast psychic thunderhead.

The female soul due to be born in 1937 was particularly sensitive and abhorred violence, perhaps because she had been killed in the First World War. This may have been the reason she decided to abort her descent and so the embryo was stillborn. However, a year later, no doubt under the pressure of karma, she was again reincarnated as a baby girl. Both descents were clearly remembered by her in later life. As if to confirm the fact, her parents gave her the name of the first stillborn child, together with the one she was christened.

In spite of her delayed descent, she was still part of that generation which would spend its childhood under wartime conditions. However, it did mean that her life was not exactly in line with the fate she might have had if she had been born at the first time round. The result was that nothing quite fitted into place for her. Her expectations were always out of joint with her situation. This, of course, might have been the lesson planned for her. Even so, several crucial opportunities to get back into sequence were lost because she chose to ignore a series of crises that confronted her and which would have put her on

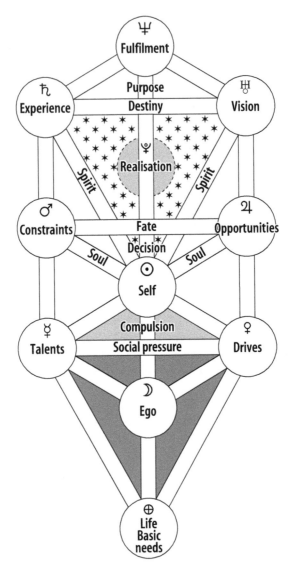

Figure 39—POSSIBILITIES
Life, it is said, is what you make it. For the kabbalistic astrologer this is a vital maxim. By contemplating one's birth chart and considering the stage one is at, it is possible to see what opportunities are open to exploit and what are not worth the effort. Many people cling on to their youthful illusions but never put them to the test because of the fear of failure, instead of finding out what is really their place in the universe. Those who use their horoscope as a guide come to see it as a map of their destiny. (Halevi.)

line again. The consequence was a life of ill health, broken relationships and great unhappiness. This is why crises should be regarded as opportunities and not impediments.

The fact that a person is intelligent does not guarantee that they will make correct choices. Some clever people believe that they know better than the Providence that places them in the best possible position to develop. After they go against the flow of evolution, they often complain that fate is cruel. This is because they refuse to acknowledge that they are directly responsible for what is happening. Sometimes a serious crisis is the only way to get such people to change direction.

If an individual is living off their Sun they can, as said, alter their fate and mitigate negative karma. Tolstoy's great novel *Resurrection* is about such an event. In this story, an aristocrat goes into moral crisis when he finds himself on the jury in a trial of a prostitute accused of murder. He recognises her as the young girl he seduced and abandoned long ago. Now she is in the gutter of society. Filled with guilt and remorse he decides to resurrect her, and himself, by going with her to Siberia where she is to serve her sentence. To his surprise, she rejects his offer to help. Out of this confrontation comes a repulsion for the idle life he has been living and a perception of the corruption in his society. The book is in fact Tolstoy's recognition of what was really going on in Tsarist Russia and how he wanted to change it, and himself, before it suffered a disastrous fate. He managed to transform his life, to a degree, by working with his peasants on his estate but the Russian empire did not change and subsequently suffered the expected revolt. This turned out to be horrific because of centuries of negative karma.

Free will allows a wide range of choices from the trivial to the fatal. It can also be perverse. Some people deliberately choose to go against the norm, swim in the other direction to evolution and even decide to be evil. Such actions inevitably generate major crises sooner or later as no one can turn the tides of the universe.

A male soul is not always born to be a man or a female soul to be a woman. Some fates are designed to correct an over-emphasis of sexuality. Thus an excessively female soul is sometimes incarnated into a masculine body, while an aggressive male soul might well be born as a girl. This can precipitate a crisis in that the individual concerned may not accept the lesson they have been given, to balance themselves and so evolve further. A similar situation sometimes comes at pubescence when both sexes are, for a time, not sure of their

Figure 40—CRISIS
Choice to expand or contract in life can also occur in a civilisation, because it
is made up of people who have some degree of free will. The Renaissance in
Europe gave the opportunity to develop. One factor was the printed book which
many could read. With the rise of literacy, new ideas and free thought began to
challenge the Church. A crisis ensued that brought on a religious and political
revolution that destroyed the atrophied medieval world view. Out of this the
modern epoch was born. (Medieval woodcut.)

orientation. They are suddenly and passionately attracted to friends of the same sex as they enter the Venusian phase. For most, such crushes soon pass but some, enjoying the buzz and excitement of adolescence, remain fixated in this sexual mode for the rest of their lives. Needless to say they, like those fated to learn what it is like to be in the opposite sex's body, will encounter much resistance from a heterosexual society. This will supply many opportunities for crisis and transformation.

Personal partnership is one of the most important areas in human relations. Here harmony and conflict are at their most intense. This is due not so much to physical factors, as most people can choose a mate sexually or, in many cultures, be matched by their families according to class, but to differences in psychological make-up. In India, the astrological compatibility is taken into account with many marriages. This is not so in the West where mutual sexual attraction, fashion, money and profession are decisive in courtship. The trouble comes after the wedding when the two psyches have to share the same space.

A husband and wife may connect physically well, through their Ascendants or Moons, but not at the soul level. One may have a Saturn square to the other's Sun causing their partner to feel hemmed in while another relationship could be blown apart by a Uranus transit that hits the Mars in both charts, leading to a serious quarrel. All these crises are useful lessons if they are handled with intelligence and knowledge.

Collective crises play an important part in history. In 1989 Saturn, Uranus and Neptune were in Capricorn, square to Mars in Libra. This combination in the sign of political order indicated that repression would be challenged by revolution and idealism. This process began with riots in Tibet and a student revolt in China's capital. Rallies in Communist Hungary were then followed by uprisings throughout the Eastern Block, culminating in the collapse of the Russian Communist regime and the break-up of the Soviet Union. During these events, people had to choose which side they supported. The vegetable masses went with the revolutionary mood of the moment while many animal level individuals, who had supported the Communist authorities, exploited the chaos to become the leaders of the emerging democratic parties by calling themselves socialists and even nationalists.

Clearly karma was being acted out, as some individuals were shot and others were discovered to be government spies, when police records were opened to the public. These events at the national and personal level stimulated crises throughout the affected countries that forced them to consider what had been happening and what they were going to do about it. Each citizen had to face the truth, sometimes about themselves and those who informed on them and about what kind of regime they wanted in the future.

A similar crisis occurred on July 14th 1789 when Venus, Jupiter and Uranus were in Leo, coming into opposition with Pluto in Aquarius. This combination was enough to set off a long-impending revolution in a Leonine France which had been on the edge of revolt against a decadent government. The ensuing chaos after the King's execution created a vacuum which Napoleon, a Leo, filled by 'picking up the crown from the gutter'. He became the nation's First Consul and then its Emperor, as France needed a royal figurehead. As the archetype of the nation, he created an expanding French empire by 'liberating' the rest of Europe in the name of the Revolution's ideals of equality and fraternity. Many people thought Napoleon was a hero, until it became obvious that he was setting up a family dynasty to govern Europe like any other conqueror.

The choice that faced the continent was whether to fight or tolerate an insane and inflated France, led by a brilliant megalomaniac. The Napoleonic wars were a major turning point for Europe. After Napoleon's defeat, the Aquarian Age was clearly seen in the rising of nationalism and the birth of Communism, which were to lead to yet more crises as the spiritual dimension of the Piscean Age had gone. This stratum of humanity was now carried on not by the state religions but various esoteric schools of the soul.

21. Schools

Not everyone is destined to be a great historic figure but anyone can develop their full potential and so find their place in the universe. To do this requires a school of the soul to teach them how. In ordinary life there are colleges and universities that train people to become cooks, architects and lawyers. However, to become a fully evolved human being requires a special kind of approach. Esoteric schools have existed throughout history in various forms from the shamans to the Masons' lodge. Many included astrology in their curriculum, alongside the particular spiritual tradition they were following. The ancient Egyptians, Greeks and Hindus had their cosmology as did the Chinese, Persians and Jews. All took into account the influences of the celestial bodies.

The Arabs, who combined Hellenic concepts with the Islamic view, developed astrology to a very high degree, in conjunction with the Jews who related it to Kabbalah. The schools of medieval Spain, especially Toledo, applied the celestial art to aid inner development. This is the tradition followed by this book. The line has been carried on into the modern era despite science all but obliterating esoteric knowledge. However, with the advent of contemporary psychology and, in particular, the work of Carl Jung, astrology has undergone a revival. With the general interest aroused during the 1960s and 70s in various spiritual disciplines, schools of the soul have made themselves known once more. This was because many people seeking higher knowledge could not find the 'Teaching' in organised religion, which had become less spiritual and increasingly social and political in outlook and content.

As regards astrology, psychology and Kabbalah, research made possible by computers revealed that, statistically, certain professions were related to particular signs while thousands of collated birth charts confirmed that the study by the ancient and medieval practitioners was quite valid. These findings attracted the attention of open-minded individuals who were also looking at alternative and

134

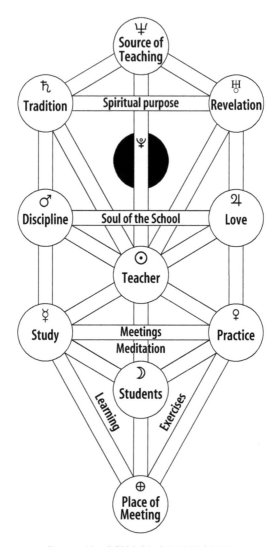

Figure 41—SCHOOL OF THE SOUL
In every culture there has always been an esoteric school that is there to aid those who wish to develop. All schools are modelled on the Tree. At the base is the place where they meet, be it a stone circle or a cathedral. The regime might be the Way of Action, Devotion or Contemplation, which relates to the thinker, feeler or doer types of people. An astrological school belongs to the Contemplative approach, as astrologers usually have a strong Mercury or Saturn in their charts. Study and practice are vital, so too are discipline and love of the subject. The inspiration or revelation of the teacher is needed if a spiritual connection with the Teaching is to be made. (Halevi.)

oriental medicine. This led to some interesting, providential encounters. An example of this phenomenon was the psychoanalyst who had her birth chart drawn up out of curiosity. As a detailed account of her mind and fate was read out, she went into shock. She then said that it had taken many years of analysis and a great deal of expense to reveal what the chart had identified within an hour.

The reason such an event could occur was not only due to the astrologer's skill but that the lady was at the point in her life at which she realised she could go no further without esoteric knowledge. She recognised that there was a limit to psychology and that now a spiritual dimension was required. Fortunately for her, a planetary transit had brought about the meeting with the astrologer who became her kabbalistic connection.

There are many organisations that say they are a school of the soul. However, they often have only a portion of the Teaching or a distorted version of it. Therefore the spiritual seeker must test any claims to esoteric knowledge against certain criteria, so as to see if what is said is genuine. For instance, some offer enlightenment on a plate when, in reality, they are out to make money or con the innocent into believing they are holders of great secrets. Some so-called schools are psychopathic *ménages* led by someone playing a power game, even believing themselves to be a spiritual master. It may take some time to find a true school but it is a sound training in how to discern a false line. Nothing should be believed until it is proven by practice. The hallmark of a real school is that it offers a solid, basic training and that its members are mature, sane and have a sense of humour.

The first stage of esoteric training is life experience. Then comes a solid grounding in the discipline to be followed, in this case astrology, psychology and Kabbalah. There is no need to learn Hebrew as kabbalistic principles are essentially universal. All that is required is to be thoroughly familiar with the basic sefirotic Tree and how the four Worlds of Jacob's Ladder integrate. As regards astrology and psychology, the same applies in that they are both systems whose language has to be learned; and this takes time.

Besides the theory of the traditions, there is practical work within a group. The introductory classes are usually led by a senior student, much to the disappointment of some people who want to go straight to the head of the school for instruction. However, much of the Teaching at this level of tuition would be lost because a beginner would not comprehend what was going on in a master class. Everyone has to start at the beginning, not only to learn the language of the tradition but to unlearn what they have learnt elsewhere, or there will be confusion. Each school has its own vocabulary and ways of doing things according to its birth chart.

Study (Mercury) and practice (Venus) are the two pillars any school stands upon. These activities manifest in learning the system and then testing it out. In the Toledo tradition, it is vital to understand the characteristics of the signs, celestial bodies and houses, their combinations, aspects and effects. With various exercises that integrate astrology, Kabbalah and psychology comes the cultivation of observation and intuition, leading to insight and prognostication. This shifts consciousness up from the conditioned reflex of the Moon mind to that of the Sun which, like its patron god Apollo, sees truth.

In Figure 41 the structure of a school of the soul is set out on the Tree. The lower part is concerned with different kinds of classes. Such meetings are not just talk and workshops but are also about creating a social and psychological vessel that no one person on their own could generate. This kind of activity widens the individuals' receptivity as they examine each others' charts, the horoscopes of well-known people and the current celestial and political climate. Running parallel to these studies are seminars on psychology and Kabbalah and inner meditations to synthesise all these traditions. Here theory and practice become discipline and love which lead to the higher levels of reason and revelation. In the esoteric application of astrological principles, the Sun of the teacher and the Moon of the students of the school give rise to a collective identity which, in turn, connects with the spiritual line of the source of the Teaching. This opens up the aim of contributing to evolution and the Divine plan.

At the everyday level, it is interesting to note that a school led by a Capricorn teacher will operate in a different way to a Pisces- or Aries-led one. This is why some people will be drawn to or put off by a particular institution. Moreover, one student will be attracted by an emotional approach, another by a practical method and yet another by an intellectual way of working. Each seeker must find the school most suited to their temperament. In addition to this, there is the formal character of any institution which is often taken into account. Some schools are philosophical, others religious and yet others occult. Some with a distinct character are usually based upon the work of some historic figure such as Solomon Ibn Gabirol, whose spirit still resides in the Pluto position of the Toledo school Tree.

Figure 42—TEACHER

One must seek out an instructor who is not only knowledgeable but worldly-wise. Many know the theory of astrology but do not understand human nature. A good teacher should be a real professional and have a sense of humour and proportion. They should not be tempted by wealth, power or sex which are the tests of leadership. A great teacher will be kind and encouraging but strict when needed and always truthful but tactful. One must not be taken in by those who claim to have secret knowledge which they never impart. (16th century woodcut.)

Ibn Gabirol was an 11th century Jewish poet and philosopher who lived in Moorish Spain. His work was carried on in the next century by Abraham Ibn Ezra, who wrote about Neo-Platonism, astrology and the Bible, besides being a poet and traveller. This line was continued throughout the Middle Ages up to Moses Cordovero, a 16th century kabbalist in Israel. He was the last teacher of traditional Kabbalah before the Lurianic line took over and the so-called Age of Reason eclipsed the psychological scheme of astrology and the mystical world-picture of Kabbalah. Fortunately, the sefirotic Tree and Jacob's Ladder were preserved and are now being updated for the present situation.

While these long-term operations of schools and lines go on, there is always the immediate circumstance to be dealt with. The most common is of social interaction or group dynamics and personal relationships. People are people and, from time to time, some very human problem that needs resolving will occur even in the most disciplined school. Here kabbalistic astrology comes into direct play. Let us examine one of the periodic episodes that happens whenever men and women come together.

22. Problems

The first lesson to be learned in any school of the soul is to be reliable. To turn up on time, attend every meeting and do all the exercises set is vital. The basis of this is that the more effort that is put in, the greater the gain. People who come late or are irregular in attendance rarely become masters of their discipline. In every session there is not only what is formally being taught but the psychological interaction between those present. As the years go by, all the moments of insight coalesce into a comprehensive understanding that someone who attends irregularly misses. This is why an esoteric school only wants candidates who are seriously committed to what is sometimes called 'The Great Work'.

One of the prerequisites for a candidate is a degree of life experience. Without knowledge of success, failure and being able to discern the true from the false, nothing new can be learned. A naïve or ignorant person cannot begin to grasp the subtleties of psychology and spirituality if they have never faced themselves. How can they discern the difference between Mercurial and Saturnian thought or Venusian passion and Jupiterian emotion? Without such discrimination they cannot comprehend astrological principles. A wide personal knowledge of the human situation is vital to comprehending the vast, divine drama in which we all play a part.

In order to accomplish this a student has to learn how to learn, which is done by absorbing lessons directly into the mind rather than by taking notes. This is because writing things down often means missing nuances that are not observed as the brain, not the psyche, records data. Kabbalistic astrology is about human nature and therefore requires an acute awareness of internal psychological dynamics as well as what goes on between people.

A typical practical exercise is that in which twelve people act out the signs of the Zodiac at an imaginary dinner party. Another is to perform a ritual dance of the Solar system and yet another a dramatised situation, such as a political negotiation where each student plays a

140

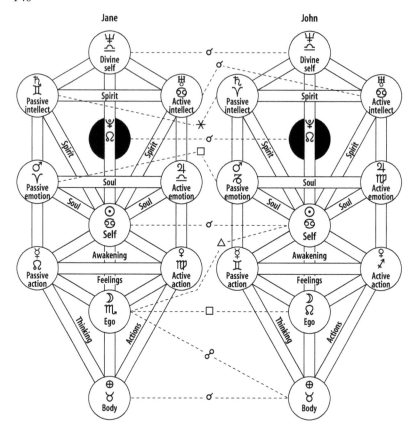

Figure 43—RELATIONSHIPS
When put on the Tree, relationships can be seen more clearly. In this case the two Suns are compatible but it might be more of a brother-sister connection. However, the Moon-egos are potentially antagonistic while the Taurean ascendant makes them physically attracted to each other. The two Mercurys can converse well but the two Venuses might mean that passion is frustrated. Fierce quarrels due to different Martial emotional settings are likely but their common Neptune means they are of the same generation group of values. John would try to dominate Jane with his Sun but her Moon would reject this approach. A lively love affair but marriage is unlikely. (Halevi.)

particular Sun-Moon combination. People then switch rôles and sides so as to see the situation from a different astrological viewpoint. For interior work an imaginary house can be visualised, based on the triads of the Tree, in which each room represents a psychological function. This is decorated and furnished according to the celestial body in that triad-sign. So for example, the thinking triad ruled by Virgo, with Mars in it, would be symbolised by a very strict and neat office while Jupiter in Virgo might produce a congenial but disorganised mess.

Besides the study of famous people's horoscopes and their biographies, there is the exercise of a group examining each member's chart in exchange for a meal in their own home. A very convivial evening can be had by all, to the benefit of the group as well as the subject, as he or she confirms or denies the accuracy of their interpretation. A senior member or tutor can then sum up and point out what has been missed and so deepen the perception of all present. Much fun can be had and a great deal learned from such exercises.

Once the art of interpreting a chart has been mastered, then the more esoteric elements can be introduced. When the chart is put on the Tree, it can reveal the unconscious part of the psyche by examining the soul, spiritual and divine triads in relation to the positions of the outer planets. This will give an insight into the special lesson of that person's fate and the purpose of their particular generation. Out of this may emerge the greater pattern into which they all fit.

In the light of this, historical periods can be examined to see how the cosmic weather has influenced certain soul groups. Turning points in the development of humanity can be identified in different cultures. With the aid of astrological computer software, charts for any period in history will reveal in the fate of nations and empires why they rose and fell or succeeded or failed in their mission. The birth charts of great heroes and villains are very informative. It is possible to see what made them outstanding and how they were partly products of their epoch. All these activities add much to an understanding of the Tree-chart as the archetypal model.

The way a school operates is also contingent upon its birth chart. If the date of its founding is known, something of its nature and fate can be discovered. There will be times when the atmosphere of the classes and groups will be tense or lax and periods when it is very lively and creative or the reverse. A wise leader or tutor will take the astrological weather into consideration and design the lessons to meet the needs of the moment. Unfortunately, not every event is predictable or controllable, especially as regards romance, passion and love.

People are attracted to each other for all sorts of reasons, ranging from pure lust to the meeting of soul mates. When such situations occur problems can arise, especially when potential lovers have partners who are not in the school. This can lead not only to the break up of marriages but to a disruption of a group as people take up positions. Such a situation has to be handled with great skill and delicacy. It is a test of a tutor's capability and an initiation for the couple and the class on how to behave according to principle and not at the personal level.

Let us take the case of John and Jane, as set out in Figure 43. John is married but his wife is not interested in self-development. She is content with her home and children. Jane, however, has been looking for her soul mate and believes John is her ideal partner because his Cancer Sun resonates with her Scorpio Moon and they both have Taurus Ascendants. This combination sparks off a very strong mutual attraction, especially in John who feels neglected at home because his wife puts their children's needs before his. Jane, who also has a Cancer Sun, feels both maternal and sexually drawn towards John. It only needed a Jupiter transit trining their Suns to trigger a romantic situation over a drink, after every class, before they went to their respective homes. One night they decided to have their *tête-à-tête* in Jane's apartment.

While John may not believe that he and Jane are soul mates, it is obvious that they get on exceptionally well at the physical and psychological levels. At last he feels his Cancer Sun is appreciated, his Leo Moon loved and his Taurus Ascendant adored. Jane, for her part, is convinced for the first time in her life that she is deeply in love as her Watery Sun and Moon respond in a release of long-pent-up passion and emotion. However, not everything is perfect. His Leo Moon is square to her Scorpio Moon and there are moments of friction when these two Fixed signs clash over him going home to his wife. Conversely, Jane reminds John of his possessive mother, also a Sun Cancer, and this arouses some traumatic memories.

During the honeymoon period of the affair, such irritations as their squared Mars' are ignored but, sooner or later, the battle as to who will dominate will have to be fought out. At this point friends in the group become concerned about the couple, who appear to be living in a psychological bubble and quite unaware of the effect their relationship is having on others. People take sides, some with painful experiences of their own, objecting to the lie being lived as regards John's wife. Others see the wider picture of the impact on the group's integrity and honesty.

When knowledge of the situation reaches the group's leader or the head of the school, John and Jane are summoned for an interview. While the tutor will not interfere with the couple's affair, he or she will point out the possible karmic result of the event. It is often at this point that one or both lovers will ask for a comment on their birth charts to see the situation and make a decision.

A readout might be done together or separately. The tutor will then examine their two charts to see the connections and what transits are going on. From this he will be able to determine what crises and tests are going on and what might come after the Jupiter trine has passed. Taking all these factors into account, the tutor may conclude that, while there are certain strong links between the two, the natal Mars square Mars in their soul triads indicates that they would eventually begin to quarrel. As for Jane's delusion of John being her soul mate, the tutor might point out to her, in private, that John was closer to being a younger brother as he was not yet a mature man. She would have to grow, to overcome her Cancerian tendency to mother and control men. No soul mate would appear until then.

What John and Jane did after such interviews would be crucial. They were no longer unaware of the karmic implications or the prognosis on their relationship if it continued to be intimate. John had a Uranus opposition coming up and this would be decisive as regards his marriage. Jane must have no part in any split if she still felt John was still the best possible partner she had met. If they were meant to be together it would happen and if not, nothing she could do would bring it about.

With this blend of astrological, psychological and kabbalistic advice, the couple might see sense and discontinue what could turn into a fatal error that would affect their future karma. Whatever the couple's decision, the situation as regards the group would be clear. This might cause John or Jane or even some members to leave the school because they put personal opinion before the universal principle.

Figure 44—SIN
In the original Hebrew this word meant 'to miss the mark'. Adam and Eve could eat anything in the Garden of Eden except from the Tree of Knowledge. The Serpent, alias Lucifer, said they could but it was they themselves who chose to eat the apple. This was their first lesson about free will and karma. The result was their descent into the physical World, to put on coats of skin; that is, to incarnate in order to begin the Great Journey of Self-realisation at the bottom of Jacob's Ladder. (Medieval woodcut.)

23. Free Will

The issue of free will has been argued about over many centuries. Some have said it does not exist as the universe is so precisely planned that there is no room for any variation. The opposite argument is that while fixed laws exist, there is a necessary degree of flexibility which allows evolution to occur. As regards the affairs of humanity, there is the choice to go with or against development. This makes mankind unique. The reason for such a position is that humanity is at the pivotal point between the highest and lowest extremes of Existence. We are the hairsprings of the cosmic mechanism that plays a crucial part in the process of SELF-realisation by being conscious of the Divine intention.

The philosophical argument for free will is that it would be pointless for humanity to be locked into a totally mechanical situation. What would be the Divine rationale for choice, if God meted out punishment and reward regardless of performance. If there were no justice, the Ten Commandments, Buddha's eightfold path and Confucius' code of conduct would make no sense. The reality appears to be that there is choice but within the limits of the human situation. Individuals and communities can make decisions which either advance or retard evolution. Karma is the check and balance of progress so that the general scheme of Evolution is affected but not put off course.

The Ten Commandments given to Moses made it very clear that free will is an important factor in history. The Israelites, who symbolised all the levels of mankind, had the option to follow the advice given, for the Commandments are not demands but recommendations. In a modern interpretation 'not to covet, lie, steal and adulterate, or there will be dire consequences' is closer to the spirit of the instructions. They are a friendly warning. The point that the evil which results will be experienced to the third and fourth generation is another issue. The word *dor* or 'generation' does not actually exist in the original Hebrew text. It was either added or replaced another word, which might have been 'lives'. It is interesting to note that many rabbis refer to the 'world to come' after death, in which reward and punishment would be given out. One kabbalistic view is that they are actually talking about reincarnation. This makes sense of many rabbinical commentaries about good and evil people getting their respective deserts. Indeed, there is more than one hint about difficulties being the result of an earlier life. In the New Testament, Jesus asked whether a man was born blind because of his own sin, implying that this affliction was the result of an action in a previous incarnation.

The concepts of Hell, Paradise and Heaven are part of every human culture, along with the belief in the transmigration of the soul from one body to another. This view was common among the Celts, the Greeks, and in the Middle East and the distant Orient. Reincarnation was part of the early Church's doctrine until it was declared a heresy in 553CE by the fifth Ecumenical Council, for various political reasons.

Esoteric astrologers, that is, those who see a birth chart as one link in a long line of fates, hold the view that the horoscope explains why people's fortunes are so different. It is clear that there is a law at work which gives this person so much talent and that person such bad luck. Metaphysically, there is no such thing as 'luck', as everything in the universe is interconnected. Even seeming accidents have, on reflection, their purpose. Some so-called mishaps are to prevent a more serious event, others to shock the person into an alert state or are the end result of a karmic process. As noted, astrological transits often occur in a fate when a decision is indicated. Such choices can reduce or enhance the potentiality contained in a birth chart. Indeed this is the main purpose of having a horoscope drawn up.

Life is made up of major and minor decisions. In many cases people choose to ignore opportunities that their fate offers them from time to time. This is because they take the easier option, rather than make an effort or take a risk. The result is that their lives are generally unexceptional. They live much the same way as millions of others in a daily and yearly round that, all too quickly for many, arrives at sad and unfulfilled old age. In contrast, those who have exploited every opportunity tend to enjoy a retirement in which they are often more active and effective than when they were working. The proverb, 'Those beloved by the gods die young', does not mean death in youth but to be still growing, exploring and expanding.

However, there are highly advanced individuals who misuse their talents, knowledge and power because they abuse the gift of free will. They are to be found, after they have fallen from Grace as a result of

Figure 45—DECISIONS
Few people find or marry their soul mate, as they are not yet mature enough to handle such teamwork. Such a meeting can only come when both are spiritually ready. Most marriages are made for different reasons. The vegetable level is instinctive while the animal is the best available in their social circle. These are rarely conscious choices. Those who wish to be fully human seek someone who at least shares the same aim to develop. This is usually corroborated by the compatibility of their charts. (16th century woodcut.)

their wilfulness, in situations where they are clearly isolated from the mainstream of life. Classic examples are the banned doctor, the unloved femme fatale and the disgraced politician. If these bitter lessons are not learnt, then the chastisement is carried over into the next life, at a yet lower level.

Sometimes the possibility of a sudden curtailment of abuse can be seen in a birth chart. James Dean, the Hollywood actor icon of youthful rebellion and star of the movie *Rebel Without a Cause*, had all the signs of self-destruction in his horoscope. He had Mars and Pluto in his 8th House of Death. And yet, despite fame and fortune, he chose to live recklessly and died in a car smash while speeding. With his great talent and appeal he could have been an important rôle-model for a generation that was being led in a trend towards disintegration by the hedonism of the drugs and free love scene. He may well have been removed by Providence before he became too potent as a negative influence on a young and naïve generation.

If an individual can recognise what is coming up in their fate by noting critical transits, then they can decide the wisest thing to do. This can only be done by those who have lifted their consciousness up from the body-Ascendant and Moon-mind to the level of the Sun or self. If a person can achieve this, then it is possible to alter fate. By this is meant that an individual can transform a destructive situation, for instance, into a creative one. Take a marital quarrel that is so nasty that it could wreck the marriage. One who knows what to expect when Mars squares Mars can carefully mitigate the tension by applying the Solar and Jupiterian principles of the soul and so avoid a conflict that could destroy the relationship. This might offset waiting for another life to heal the damage done.

Take the situation of a beautiful young woman who had two suitors. One was a poor but lively writer whom she loved and the other a dull but comfortably well-off academic. As a Cancerian, she wanted a secure home and children and so she chose the safe life of a university city. She had her children and nice house but still secretly yearned for the novelist, who later became a well-known author. Had she chosen him, her life would have been a struggle but very rich in experience. She missed marrying her soul mate and a chance to accelerate her development.

Fate is not about marrying a particular person, as at least three potential partners can provide the lesson to be learned. As regards relationships, most people respond to a physical or psychological archetype related to their own astrological make-up. Earth and Water individuals attract each other as do Air and Fire signs. However, on what level the partnership will operate depends upon whether the Ascendant, Moon or Sun is dominant. Some will be drawn by a body type and others to a social persona, like the man who said his second wife looked and acted like his first spouse but had a quite different temperament. Relationships at the Solar or soul level are quite rare. One has to be a full individual to recognise another of the same calibre. Most memorable love affairs are either pure sex, a fantasy projection or a mixture of both.

It does sometimes happen that a man and a woman who are at the same point of development when they meet have a sense that they are very familiar to each other. It is as if they already know each other. This may well be the case. It does not necessarily mean they are soul mates, although they might well marry. They can both belong to the same soul group or have had a relationship in a previous life. Either way, such an encounter is often fatal in the sense that they have a lifetime connection or have a specific mission to carry out mutually. Such events can only occur when people have reached a Solar level of development.

24. Development

The process of human development takes a very long time. Indeed, some esoteric astrologers say that individuals have to incarnate under each sign in order to experience all the zodiacal archetypes. One's destiny may be to act as a healer, soldier or trader in every life but it will be from twelve different psychological angles. After several circuits of the Zodiac a person must inevitably become increasingly familiar with human condition. This order of experience marks out an old and wise soul. However, it is not necessary to go through an endless zodiacal wheel to gain such knowledge if one chooses to follow the path of conscious development which turns the cycle into an ascending spiral. Schools of the soul, as said, provide a training that can shorten the process of maturation and accelerate individual evolution.

In a school that follows the astrological-kabbalistic tradition, the discipline is to use the birth chart to develop. In this approach the student observes the tendencies of their horoscope, seeking to master, modify and improve their performance as well as take maximum advantage of every astrological transit.

The first phase of development is to control the Ascendant. In this exercise the characteristics of the sign and its element are closely observed and refined. For example, someone with a Fiery Ascendant would have to learn how not to follow an instant response to every situation. In contrast, a Watery Ascendant would need to overcome a strong impulse to withdraw while an Earthy Ascendant would have to be trained in how to be more emotionally sensitive and an Airy Ascendant learn to be more practical. All would have to be particularly aware whenever there was a strong trine, square or opposition to the Ascendant that would stimulate instinctive reactions.

The Moon, which symbolises the ever-changing lower mind, continually acts out its conditioning. This has to be observed very closely in order to perceive just how much thought, feeling and action is ruled by the sign and House the Moon occupies. This requires very strict attention. Once the best and worst characteristics of the Moon

151

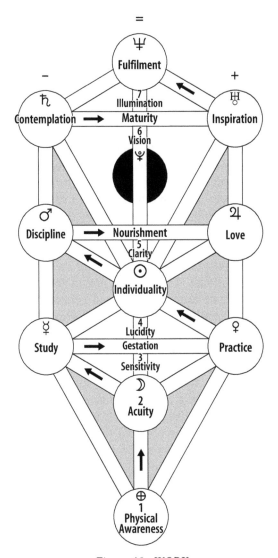

Figure 46—WORK
Development requires effort and a method. Using kabbalistic astrology as the mode, one first considers the Ascendant as a clue to how to relate to physicality; then the Moon-ego and its House. Mercury's position will give insight into mental processes and Venus the vitality available. Understanding the sign and House of the Sun, or self, is crucial because this is the centre of our psychological Solar system. Mars and Jupiter and their configurations will reveal the soul loading while Saturn and Uranus indicate how the transpersonal operates in the chart. Neptune and Pluto's positions point out the aim of that incarnation. (Halevi.)

mind have been identified, then the Lunar persona can be trained to be a good servant or actor who can play a set of rôles. In everyday life, certain situations require particular masks. These are usually reflexes. However, conscious control enables one to deal with a circumstance in a new way which opens up wider possibilities. This leads to development that can alter the mechanical pattern of fate.

Such a mastery of the Lunar ego reveals that the mind is made up of many sub-personalities. Some of these are easily recognisable but others will have been largely unconscious up to that point of development. A study of the Tree-chart can help identify these habitual tendencies and attitudes by noting what is in the various triads and their astrological aspects to each other. Take, for example, an afflicted Mercury in Scorpio which would place it in the passive emotional triad. This would make the person extremely critical, resulting in the quite unconscious, barked comment that would hurt not only others but themself in that people would steer clear of them. This could be a crucial factor in their fate. Likewise Venus in the same sign, well aspected, could mitigate any sharpness and generate a sensuous but disciplined sub-personality. This too could greatly influence that individual's life.

As regards the Sun, continuous effort is made to perceive fate from the level of the self. This means constantly supervising the ego-Moon and the Mercury-Venus functions while being aware of what sub-personalities are influencing one's conduct and attitudes. By being well acquainted with one's Tree-chart it is possible to control compulsions and adjust to the ebb and flow of circumstance, like a skilful sailor. If the conscious part of the psyche is brought under control, then the more subtle principles of the mind can be accessed, studied and eventually mastered. Thus the first four stages of physical awareness, acuity, sensitivity and lucidity pave the way for a clarity of the soul and beyond (see Figure 46).

The paths that compose the Sun, Mars and Jupiter triad of the soul are shared with the emotional and conceptual triads of the Tree-chart. These store the largely unconscious contents of the mind which are the result of this life's experience and karma. Deep inside every individual are myriad memories and psychological associations. Some are easily identifiable, like certain fixed views and emotional responses. Those that are not are either experiences and complexes that have all but been forgotten or repressed for some reason. Nevertheless, they have an influence on how one regards the world.

153

Figure 47—TRANSFORMATION
Scorpio is the sign directly concerned with transformation. Its symbol is also an eagle, indicating the possibility of shift from a lower dimension to a higher one. Eagles are creatures of the Air, signifying spirit. A change can only occur when the Sun-self activates Saturn, Uranus and Pluto of the Great Triad of the spirit through awareness of the cosmos. The Sun is the key because it is in the place where the three upper Worlds meet. The lowest aspect of self is at the Crown of the body while its middle focus is at the heart of the psychological Tree. The spiritual dimension of the self is at the bottom of the Tree of Creation. The art is to fuse them into one by conscious effort. (Graphic by Halevi.)

For example, someone may be quite unaware of a deep anger which they emanate that puts people off. This could be seen in Mars in Capricorn in the 8th House. Such a combination may be due to some injustice in this life, deliberately forgotten, or in a previous incarnation. The power of such a negative emotion could affect all the left-hand triads on the psychological Tree to such a degree that it could become an unconscious obsession.

Such a mental affliction could mar that person's professional and private life, until it was pointed out by a good and courageous friend, a competent psychoanalyst or a wise astrologer. This event would probably occur during a Mars or Saturn transit that brought the tendency to light and crisis. Then would come the decision to deal with the problem or not. Here is where a psychological or spiritual discipline can help.

Should the individual decide that their problem was not that important because they could not be bothered or were too frightened to acknowledge their anger, then little could be done. If they were at the vegetable level, they would go on to repeat their pattern so that their fate would be quite mechanical. The result would be a predictable form according to their typology and external circumstance, like the person who follows in their parents' footsteps and is an archetypal model of whatever stage they are at in their culture. The old peasant and the aristocrat are classical examples.

If the person with the anger problem is at the animal level, then the Mars in Capricorn in the 8th House might manifest in a ruthless approach to life. Such an individual could make a brilliant prosecuting lawyer, military commander or butcher. All these and similar occupations concerned with controlled and justified violence would allow a release for the unconscious anger. However, in an intimate relationship, such a need might destroy any possibility for a permanent partnership. Here again fate would be determined by an unconscious compulsion.

In the case of an individual trying to be fully human, an honest recognition of the problem that could dominate a life is vital. By understanding the mechanism of the dynamics and structure of the psyche as loaded by the birth chart, it would be possible consciously to compensate and eventually eliminate the anger by directing it into more creative activities. This would be done by the practice of various disciplines such as fencing, Tai Chi or an artistic expression that would defuse and soften the hidden rage until it could be used to transform the person's being.

The Tree of Figure 46 sets out the programme of development. Here each celestial principle is applied to raise the level of consciousness. Knowing where each is placed in the Zodiac and the houses can help to adjust and exploit the particular functions. This is what development and transformation is about.

Figure 48—GRACE
When one begins consciously to live out one's birth chart, many new things start to happen. What were once seen as misfortunes become tough but vital lessons. The good things are no longer perceived as luck, or the result of a harmonious transit, but gifts of Providence. Fate takes on a totally different dimension when viewed as a well-designed plan. There are also moments of Grace, in which a situation or teacher gives an insight into what this particular life is about. (Robert Fludd, 17th century.)

25. *Transformation*

When people begin to walk the path of self-realisation, certain changes start to occur. For those who follow the astrological-kabbalistic method, these manifest in the increased awareness of their Tree-chart as an integral element in their life. It becomes, in time, a major point of reference as they perceive their progress as a part of human evolution. As each birthday comes round, so the student takes into account the celestial situation at the moment when the Sun returns to its zodiacal position at the time they were born. By doing this they may perceive the extraordinary system of coincidences that put them in exactly the right place and time for their development. They will, moreover, become well aware of how all the people they know are relevant to their fate because of their astrological connections.

With this order of observation, every significant incident takes on a coherent meaning. This is also seen in regard to contemporaries whose lives run parallel to their own. While people born into the same generation share many similar experiences, each individual will view events according to their personal astrological make-up and level. As time goes on, this leads to an insight as to why different kinds of fate unfold despite a common, general, astrological and historical background. Here is where inner transformation separates out, as the Bible puts it, 'the sheep from the goats'.

Those at the vegetable stage of development, upon reaching their physical peak, generally begin a gradual decline until they become ageing bodies with childlike minds. This kind of transformation belongs to the natural world where every organism will die having completed its species' life cycle. And yet even vegetable people have the opportunity to shift level if they take up the challenge of the Uranus opposition around the age of forty. Unfortunately, some men take up with girls half their age in an attempt to prove they are still young and vigorous while career women suddenly want to settle down and have children for similar reasons. Alas, for most these options are not a solution and they will have to face the reality of

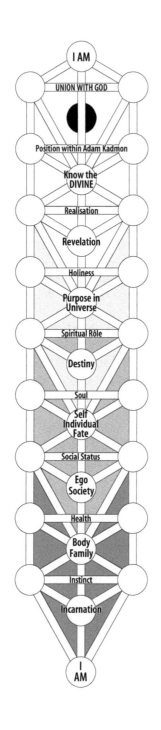

mortality, unless there is a profound interior transformation of attitude; which can happen. No human being is ever without this choice.

The animal level individual has a better chance to change his life into something more than prolonging his prime. The Uranus opposition can make him review his fate and decide to change its course. This requires a degree of maturity that takes into account what is really of value. Many, to their surprise upon reflection, realise that this is not necessarily fame or fortune. One woman discovered a love of gardening while a man wanted more time to paint as he had always wanted to be an artist. Both these activities opened up the possibility of development and transformation.

A classic example of this phenomenon was Heinrich Schliemann, a Capricornian businessman. After making a fortune he retired at the age of forty-six so that he could devote all his time and money to archaeology and history, which Capricorn loves. In the face of much criticism from scholars, he believed he knew where the site of Troy could be found. Much to the annoyance of the professional archaeologists, he discovered the remains of an ancient city. Whether or not it was Troy is a question of learnèd debate. Much more important was that Schliemann had not only altered his fate, which in a lesser man would have been to become an ever-weakening competitor in the business market, but found his destiny. His discoveries opened up a whole new facet of history. He proved that legends were not just romantic fantasies. From his time on, archaeologists began to look at classical texts and scriptures in a new way.

Those who work on their birth chart and exploit the latent talent contained in it, based upon what has been learnt, often retain a youthful sparkle that even shines through the wrinkles of old age. Such people are still very much interested in life but not from a worldly point of view. Many live full lives without leaving their homes because the internal and higher realms interest them more. Such still young-at-heart souls continually ponder the lessons of their lives and observe current affairs from a very wide and long-term perspective. This is the

Figure 49 (Left)—ASCENT
In this Jacob's Ladder the degrees of development are shown in various stages. The lower levels are about the experience of incarnation while the middle section is concerned with psychological development. The upper reaches of the Ladder are beyond most people but one can get an insight into what the higher levels of humanity are seeking to accomplish. The topmost area is about the ultimate return of the individual and mankind to Adam Kadmon. (Halevi.)

Saturnian stage of development when the pattern of personal and general events are seen very clearly in retrospect.

These so-called 'retired' people, who are still physically active, often devote much time and money to helping others and participating in all sorts of projects. Here is where the wealth or experience they have acquired is made full use of. As one sixty-year-old entrepreneur observed, 'I now know what my life is really about'. This man, with Sun in Leo and Moon in Capricorn, organised a series of tours to the Holy Land, Spain and other sacred places as well as setting up an international conference on Kabbalah at Oxford. Indeed, he remarked that these projects had redeemed a relentless business career. Such a reflection indicated that his soul had awakened and he had been transformed from a ruthless animal man into a considerate human being.

For those who have attained the human status, there is much work to be done to spread the light of esoteric knowledge. For example, a seemingly academic operation run by a woman of over ninety, with Sun in Gemini and Moon in Sagittarius, published a journal on sacred subjects that was read worldwide. Its contributors included princes, professors and others, who put forward a spiritual perspective not found in other international learnèd magazines. The aim was to maintain the light of civilisation in a world in which the finer values of life were being eclipsed by a materialistic culture. Such enterprises cannot be carried out by the conventional media which are at the mercy of commerce. Only those with vision can execute these kind of operations. They are usually advanced souls who have volunteered to incarnate so as to carry out such missions.

This requires that they are born at just the right time so as to be at the height of their powers when their particular talent is needed. An example of this was the Russian writer and philosopher, Peter Ouspensky, who brought the esoteric teaching of George Gurdjieff to the West after the Bolshevik revolution which destroyed any possibility of his nation's progress for decades. Ouspensky was a Sun Pisces and Moon Virgo. This gave him a feeling for the mystical and the precision to set a complex metaphysical system down in an intelligible form. Ouspensky's books were directly and indirectly responsible for schools of the soul being set up all over the world. They prepared the ground for the revival of interest in esoteric knowledge after the two most destructive wars ever seen on the planet. These had been foreseen and so a modern version of the Teaching had to be spread globally in case Western Civilisation was destroyed. This brings us to how prophecy is possible from an astrological and kabbalistic viewpoint.

26. Nemesis

The First World War began when the Austro-Hungarian Archduke Franz Ferdinand, heir to the empire's throne, was assassinated in 1914. At that time there was great political tension between the major European powers as to who would dominate the continent. This was being brought to a head by Mars (war) in Leo (imperialism) opposing Jupiter (power) and Uranus in Aquarius (radical political action) as Pluto (nemesis) was about to enter Cancer (community). This configuration was to precipitate an arms race and an inevitable clash. However, some local incident was needed to trigger a confrontation that would release a massive landslide of European karma.

The Archduke had gone to the Balkans, the centre of much ethnic tension, on a goodwill mission. As he and his wife were driven through the crowded streets of Sarajevo, a Serb nationalist threw a bomb at their car but they escaped without harm. This occurred as the Archduke's natal Mars was squared by Mars' transiting position in his 8th House of Death while Saturn conjoined his natal Uranus on his Descendent and opposed his Sun. This configuration indicated a sudden fatal affliction of his health in a public place.

Having avoided this assault, the Archduke took another route. Unfortunately his driver, being unfamiliar with the town, slowed down to make a turn, just where another Serbian nationalist, Gavrilo Princip, happened to be standing. He grabbed the opportunity to shoot the Archduke and his wife dead. This started the First World War. Austria set out to punish Serbia which caused Russia, Serbia's ally, to step in to protect their Slavic brothers. Germany then joined Austria against Russia, who called upon France and Britain for support as they were part of an alliance designed to offset Germany's growing military might. Within days, millions of men put on uniforms in a wave of war hysteria to fight the image of an evil enemy created by their government propaganda.

When there is such a collective mood, the individual is of little account. The vegetable masses, on all sides, were told they would be defending their homes and families, which aroused their blood, while animal level people were excited by the possibility of being heroes or opportunity to make money. Those of the human level either refused to be part of such madness or joined the forces to act as a sane element in the rising chaos.

The astrological situation in the summer of 1914 pivoted upon Pluto in one degree of Cancer, the sign of the family and the masses of humanity. This planet of death, rebirth and transformation was to remain in Cancer until 1939, when the Second World War began. During this time, Europe and the world underwent tremendous political and social changes that were to destroy the Continent's position as the world leader of civilisation.

Such a dreadful reckoning came about because of the bad karma that had been accumulating since the Europeans first started to explore and exploit the rest of the world from the 15th century onwards. The last time Pluto had been in this sign was in the 17th century when there had been a number of fierce wars over which European nation should control certain areas of the globe. Germany, a latecomer to empire building, wanted its portion of the world and set out to compete with its rivals on equal if not superior military terms. Unfortunately, when a cosmic storm cloud is about to burst, some individuals and nations believe that with the discharge of tension they can ride on the release and accomplish anything. Germany had a long prepared plan to invade France while the French were convinced they could regain the provinces lost to Germany in 1871. Meanwhile imperial Russia, on the edge of revolution, needed a foreign diversion to redirect the attention of the masses. Britain, then just past its peak as the world's leading power, felt it a matter of honour to defend little Belgium, which had been overrun by the German 'Hun'.

Such ambitions, based upon delusions, had to come to a head as Saturn conjoined Pluto in Cancer after being squared by Mars in Libra in August 1914. Mars then entered Scorpio, following Venus, and squared Jupiter and Uranus in Aquarius. Such a thunderhead could only generate great destruction or creation. In this case there was more of the former than the latter.

At the personal level each individual contributes something to their community's karma by the way they live out their fate. Many British people, for example, accepted the benefits of their empire without considering the cost to their overseas subjects. African tribal lands had been appropriated and cheap labour in India was taken for granted. In

Figure 50—NEMESIS
This cartoon sums up the European situation prior to the Fist World War. Each empire, fired up by nationalism, generated a fierce rivalry as Pluto entered Cancer, indicating a destructive period in the Western family's unity. In August 1914, Mars entered Libra and squared Pluto, before moving into Scorpio. Meanwhile, Saturn conjoined Pluto and squared Mars. All this celestial configuration manifested in the Great War that changed the continent. Such a devastating conflict tore off the persona of a high culture that made Europeans believe they were the world's leaders. (Graphic by Frederick Rose, pre 1914.)

Tasmania the native population had been wiped out like vermin. All these things had been perpetrated by individual Britons and accepted by most people at home as the norm. When one Englishwoman had protested at the British invention of the concentration camp during the Boer War, she had been seen as a traitor.

If a country has no spiritual core, it will inevitably drift into disaster. The function of civilisation is to raise the quality of life and give guidance to the nation. Unfortunately the religious, political and cultural establishments of the European nations of the time were no more than power-oriented organisations. This is because the esoteric aspect of life had been all but forgotten. The Bible states, 'without vision the people perish' and so it was as Pluto passed through Cancer. As it entered Leo in 1939, it was clear that a bitter lesson had not been learnt. The inter-war years had seen the rise of dictatorship, Fascism and Communism. At that point the Lunar Nodes were squared to Pluto as Saturn conjoined the Dragon's Tail in Taurus, exactly on Adolf Hitler's Sun—and so he became the instrument of Europe's second devastation.

After the Second World War there was a revival of interest in esoterica. This occurred when the 'Baby Boom' generation, born when Neptune, the principle of the Divine, was moving through Libra, reached adulthood. No doubt many in this generation had been killed in the war. While some set out to enjoy their cut-off youth, others sought to find out what life was really about. This was when the Ark of the Teaching was open again, having survived the flood of global conflict.

Many spiritual traditions and schools of the soul that had been discreetly hidden in wartime came out into the open. The revival of astrology and interest in Kabbalah were among these movements. Such was the enthusiasm for astrology that not a few commercial companies used it to select staff and predict the patterns of the stock market, aided by the computer's ability to calculate charts quickly.

More significantly, astrology began to be applied to personal psychology as counsellors dealing with the break-up of the family, caused by Uranus passing through Libra, the sign of marriage, had to cope with an increased influx of clients. At the next level, astrology became extremely useful as part of many spiritual disciplines, including Kabbalah. As we have seen, strengths and weaknesses can be identified and psychological fault lines corrected. Moreover, latent potentialities could be brought out and developed in conjunction with the ebb and flow of the cosmos. Here we come to the subject of 'Providence' which anyone who is involved with spiritual work knows is a vital element in what is sometimes seen as mere coincidence.

27. Providence

The origin of the word 'Providence' means to foresee and to provide for the present and future. It is generally recognised as an extraordinary event that comes 'out of the blue'. That last word, symbolising the sky or Heaven, indicates the celestial factor at work. In fact it operates all the time. If the Earth were a little too near or far from the Sun, organic life could not survive. Moreover, the tilt of the planet is exactly right for the seasons to unfold and various climatic zones to exist to support different species. Within the ecological scheme, every creature has its niche, be it the smallest microbe or the largest whale. This is general Providence that takes care of the overall flow of Evolution.

Human beings are given bodies at birth that contain all the instinctive knowledge gained over millions of years. This physical vehicle is the most sophisticated organism on the Earth. It not only performs all manner of mechanical, chemical and electronic processes but allows the person to perceive the material world through the five senses. What better instrument and vehicle could one be provided with. The brain alone is a masterpiece of engineering. It permits individuals to develop a wide range of skills, emotions and thoughts that gave rise to science, art, philosophy and religion as well as the basic abilities to exist in almost any part of the planet. The reason for this is that humanity has a special function in the Divine scheme. This is, as said, to be the self-conscious agent of the Absolute in the midst of Existence.

It was said, in the opening chapters, that Existence is a vast mirror in which God can behold God. Mankind is the organ of perception of Adam Kadmon, by which the Absolute explores every aspect of the universe. Each individual is a microcosmic Adam and as such is the principle of consciousness, by which the self reflects upon the SELF in the macrocosm of Existence.

The process of self-realisation within a human being takes many lives but gradually there is an ascent from the lowest instinctive vegetable level up the scale of Jacob's Ladder to the culmination or

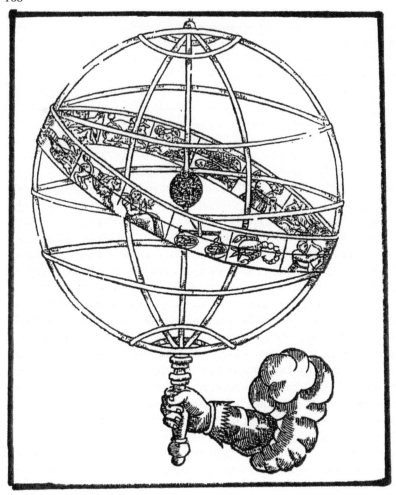

Figure 51 — PROVIDENCE
Like Nature, the fate of the masses is general. Individuals do not count. According to esoteric tradition there are, however, the Watchers, discarnate humans of advanced development, who look after special groups and people who merit it. These guardians protect and provide but do not interfere with general evolution. However, they help design the fate of advanced individuals about to reincarnate. A birth chart is a progress report and instruction on what to do when they reach maturity. This destiny is part of the Divine Plan, guided by the Hand of God. (16th century print.)

reunion with the Divine, spoken of by many spiritual traditions. Through this process each person, with their soul mate, returns to their place in Adam Kadmon. Destiny is the particular function by which individuals find their way back to their origin while carrying out their unique task.

In order for anyone to fulfil their mission or destiny, it is necessary to undergo a prolonged course of training. During this process, which takes many incarnations, many lessons and skills have to be learned. Providence provides the teachers and the classes. These may take the form of parental figures and specially designed situations through the process of karma. The horoscope reveals just how precisely things are organised so that people will be in the best place to learn what they need to know for their current stage and incarnation.

Having been born and given a certain fate that will grant the maximum possibilities to develop, people are monitored by discarnate mentors, besides those who are embodied at the same time. These invisible instructors have been recognised in many ancient cultures. Some call them the Ancestors and others guardian angels. Socrates referred to his unseen helper as his daemon. Many individuals think of them as inner teachers while others have regarded them as their guiding genius.

In childhood, most children are watched over by their parents. However, occasionally a boy or girl is saved by some kind of outside intervention as they blunder innocently into danger. Most of us can remember an incident, while out on our own on some adventure, in which we missed death by millimetres or seconds because something odd happened that made us stop or jump. Most regard this as just luck but those who are wise or experienced see such events as providential intervention. Such events are often triggered by a transit like a Mars-Uranus conjunction. This indicates that an accident-prone time is imminent. If a person is alert, they will recognise an odd synchronistic incident that warns them to be extra-careful. These kind of happenings can take many forms. Some are highly unusual and others seemingly quite natural.

An example of the former was the woman on the edge of a nervous breakdown who met her first lover, whom she had not seen for twenty years, 'by chance' in a town neither had ever been into before. This encounter saved her sanity as memories of good times were discussed. In the latter case, during the war, a sailor caught a sudden chill which meant he was left behind on shore. His warship, guarding convoys out in the Atlantic, was sunk with only five survivors. Both these people were on the path of inner development.

According to Kabbalah, such episodes are contrived by what are called *Maggidim* or Watchers. These are discarnate people who are usually of a similar type to those they watch over but a stage further in psychological or spiritual evolution. They have the task of instructing as well as protecting their charges by carefully stage-managing events, such as getting certain people together or directing a person to a junk shop where they would find the out-of-print book they need. This is not as difficult as it seems, if life is seen as a theatrical production. For example two people, who would learn much from each other, could find themselves sitting together on a long flight. This is easily arranged by psychically nudging airline personnel to give certain passengers particular seats. Many people can recall a seemingly random decision that led to an important opportunity. At the time an odd feeling of being guided is often experienced but only remembered after the event. A negative parallel is when one is being unconsciously psychologically manipulated by a lover or enemy. The only difference is that you can see them.

As said, astrological transits can create the conditions and mood that bring about certain situations. One example is the first encounter with a future personal or professional partner. Any transit relating to the 7th House, or its ruler, will make an individual receptive to such a possibility. Someone at work, or in the social scene, will suddenly catch the attention. If they are affected by a similar transit, then an unexpected romance or work relationship can begin. Whether it will last beyond the transit's period is another matter. Such events can be a long-planned fatal event, detectable in a birth chart or what is called a 'set up'. That is an incident specially organised by the Maggidim to help the process of development.

Let us examine an example of both cases in one event. In October 1492 Pluto was in Scorpio, the sign of hidden things, and in conjunction with Mercury, the planet of the explorer, while the Moon's Node, also in Scorpio, indicated a general transformation of the perception of the world. This was the month in which Columbus discovered the Americas, starting a global process of millions of Europeans and Africans flooding into the newly discovered continent. Columbus was a man of destiny. He underwent a thorough training as a sailor and sea captain before he began to seek a patron to back his vision of a Western route to China and India. He had many tests to pass that strengthened his resolve. However, after many years of trailing around the courts of Europe to raise cash for ships, just when he was about to give up the Queen of Spain suddenly offered him support. What made her reverse her previous decision is unknown but something prompted her to finance Columbus, even if it meant pawning her own jewels. Here was a fatal commitment that allowed the New World to be discovered. Some might say that the result was a disaster, since millions of native Americans died of Old World diseases as well as war and being overworked by the Spanish and Portuguese. But from a global perspective, the civilisations of the Incas and Aztecs had become decadent and needed an additional stimulus to move evolution on. The brutal sacrifice of tens of thousands of prisoners of war on Mexican altars horrified even the toughest Spanish soldiers. Something had to stop and start again anew.

Many of the native Americans who died were soon reborn, either as pure Indians, as they were miscalled, or as half-white or half-black as the three races mixed. This generated a new and vital gene-pool and a combination of cultures that would blossom in the distant future. In the British colonies the Africans were eventually freed from slavery and their descendants were to lead the way towards a collective consciousness that influenced Blacks world wide.

If one looks at history at this cosmic level, many seemingly senseless events fall into place. The Roman Empire appeared initially to the Celts as a deadly enemy. However, Rome raised their tribal culture to a level of civilisation. Without this transformation, Christianity, Greek philosophy and all that makes the Western world unique could not have occurred. Again, if the West had never come into being, there would have been no progress in many fields that have furthered human evolution.

Unfortunately, as noted, not all advanced souls are concerned with the good of humanity. Some people of destiny can not only exploit the less intelligent but distort the course of a nation's evolution if it is in a state of crisis, as Germany was in the 1930s. Adolf Hitler and Rudolph Steiner were both people of destiny, one of darkness and one of light, who were to take part in the endless fight between good and evil.

172

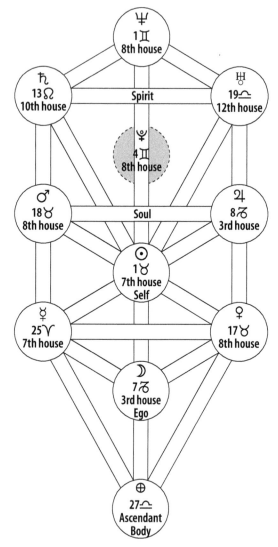

Figure 52—ADOLF HITLER
This was a man obsessed by power. But, because of his evil nature, he led a
defeated and humiliated Germany into a second, more devastating war. This was
possible because Germany is ruled by Scorpio and Taurus and Hitler's chart with
Sun, Venus and Mars in Taurus brought out the nation's shadow side of Scorpio.
Saturn in Leo in the 10th House and the Moon in Capricorn gave Hitler the
ambition to lead a people seeking revenge resulting in Scorpionic self destruction.
In the face of defeat, Hitler committed suicide after saying Germany should be
destroyed because it had failed him. (Halevi.)

28. *Destiny*

Germany is said to be a Scorpionic and Taurean nation. This is based upon its northern and southern characters which tore Germany apart during the Reformation, when the strict Prussian form of Protestantism opposed the more Venusian, Taurean version of Catholicism. Bismarck, the 19th century Chancellor, unified the nation with his policy of 'Blood and Iron'. Unfortunately, this imperial tendency, stemming from a mixture of the Plutonian military and a Taurean desire to acquire more territory, resulted in the defeat of Germany in the First World War. The humiliation of this potentially great nation generated the enormous anger and desire for revenge common to frustrated Taureans and Scorpios.

Adolf Hitler, the son of a customs official, believed that he and Germany had a great destiny. However, he was not interested in the great music, philosophy and science of the country but its rôle as the leading power of the world. He based his view on the pre-Christian warrior culture which had defeated the Romans. His ideal was a modern nation of Aryan supermen and women, the *Herrenvolk,* who would dominate what he saw as a decadent Judeo-Christian Europe.

Hitler had Saturn in Leo in the 10th House, which made him excessively ambitious, with Jupiter conjunct Moon in Capricorn. This gave him Napoleon's aspirations. Neptune and Pluto in Gemini in the 8th House may well have given him the notion that he was destined to achieve greatness, despite his initial setback to become a famous artist. Mars conjunct Venus in Taurus, together with the Sun in the 7th House, no doubt contributed to the delusion that he and Germany had an historic partnership.

Hitler's fantasy was confirmed in his own mind when he escaped being killed by a shell during the Great War, in which he attained the rank of corporal. When he found he could rabble-rouse the bitter and discontented unemployed on the streets, he believed he had discovered his path of destiny. In a Germany suffering from a punitive peace treaty it only needed someone to voice the deep Scorpionic resentment most people felt. Hitler soon rose to be a master orator of hate, especially against the Jews and Communists whom he accused of betraying Germany. In a nation looking for a scapegoat, the Jews were the perfect target as aliens. This trend was an inherent part of Christian culture that each Easter portrayed Jews as Christ killers.

Hitler became the shadow side of both the Scorpionic and Taurean aspects of Germany. He promised to restore the nation's dignity through the Nazi party's propaganda machine. This ploy convinced many, discontented with the weak government and sick of the ensuing chaos, that Hitler was the strong leader they needed to fill the vacuum of the abdicated Kaiser. He was voted in to become Chancellor in January 1933 as the Sun conjoined his Jupiter and Moon.

The desire for a strong father figure to lead the nation out of its mire caught the German imagination. From here on few argued with re-armament, which got rid of unemployment, or the blatant murder of Hitler's political rivals, dissidents and Jews. So it was that, by 1939, Nazi Germany was ready to begin the war Hitler had long planned. Its aim was to attack Poland and eventually invade the Soviet Union, with the view of expanding Germany's living space. As Saturn conjoined Hitler's Sun, Germany became totally identified with its leader's destiny. Its people cheered at its easy victories over the Low Countries and France and the exclusion of Britain from the Continent. However, in 1942 as Saturn conjoined Uranus in Taurus, there was the first sign of limits being put on Hitler's ambition. That summer his previously successful military machine suffered two major defeats at the hands of the British and Russians. From that time on the Germans were in retreat until 1945 when, in the face of defeat, as Saturn opposed Hitler's Jupiter and Moon, he blew his brains out in a Berlin bunker.

The lesson here is that the fate of the vegetable masses can be bound to an evil person of destiny. Moreover, few animal level people can resist the seductive glamour of power. Only those who have individuated to a degree can perceive history objectively and act accordingly.

Steiner, like Hitler, was of humble origin. He rose to be a positive man of destiny because of his clearly karmic accumulation of higher knowledge. He was an authority on the poet-philosopher Goethe, of whom, some say, he was a reincarnation, returned to finish his mission. Steiner, however, was not only a leading scholar but a thinker and visionary in his own right. With Sun in Pisces, Saturn in

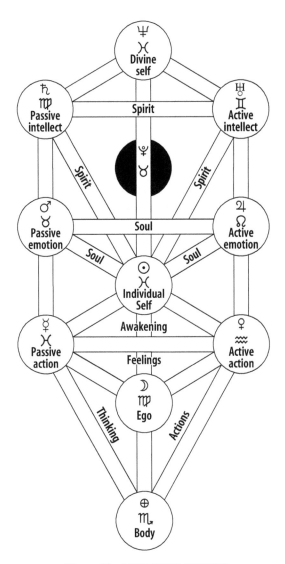

Figure 53—RUDOLPH STEINER
This was a man from the same culture as Hitler but he was keyed into the spiritual dimension. As a Piscean, Steiner had a visionary insight into the esoteric teaching of the Theosophical Society. He led a movement which became an important influence in the early 20th century. This was the positive aspect of Germany which had a tradition of mystics, such as Hildegard of Bingen, Meister Eckhart and Jacob Böhme, as well as a strong alchemical and Masonic heritage. If the Germans had heeded Steiner, then war might have been avoided. Here is the factor of free will at the personal and general level. (Halevi.)

Virgo and a Scorpio Ascendant, he had an unusual spiritual capability that could also be very practical. This was seen in his scientific as well as mystical approach with a touch of genius given by Uranus being in Gemini. Such a combination indicated that his work would be an important influence on the esoteric community.

In 1912-13 when Mars opposed his Uranus, indicating a time of decision, and Jupiter in Sagittarius squared his Mercury, he broke with the Theosophical Society, of which he was an important member. He then founded his own school of the soul, the Anthroposophical Society. This organisation developed a wide programme that introduced esoteric ideas and methods into science, art and education. Steiner put forward a metaphysical view of Existence that took into account ancient concepts about the universe and psychology. He maintained that the soul as well as the brain of a child should be trained. Many, dissatisfied with organised religion and mechanistic science, were attracted by his approach which became part of Western culture.

It is said there are usually three candidates for a particular mission, in case the first or second fail because of human weakness. King George VI of Britain was the second option, as his brother Edward chose to wed an American divorcée rather than be king. Edward had Mars in Aries which made him somewhat impetuous and thoughtless. Here Providence may have intervened, as Edward was not the kind of monarch Britain needed at this point in history. When George was crowned on May 12th 1937, Mars was conjoining his natal Mars in Sagittarius. This indicated that his reign would include global conflict. Indeed the Second World War broke out in 1939.

As a quiet and disciplined naval officer who had experienced battle in the First Great War, he was the perfect stoic figurehead, in contrast to the Fiery Winston Churchill, his Prime Minister. Together they became the poles of restraint and inspiration that Britain required to survive. Without them the nation might have suffered defeat and invasion, which would have put an end to European civilisation.

Throughout history, people of destiny have been crucial to the development of humanity. These individuals have not always been obvious heroes and heroines, or even known for what they have done but, without doubt, each at their level has contributed to the whole. The first nomad who planted a seed and settled down to cultivate and harvest it transformed mankind into farmers, while the inventor of the wheel was as great as Leonardo da Vinci.

Nations, as noted, also have a mission to carry out. Let us examine the destiny of one of the oldest Western nations, England, by consulting its birth chart.

178

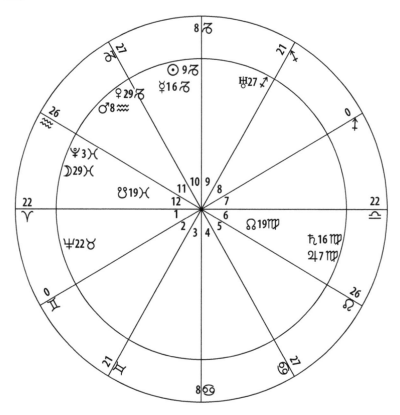

Figure 54—ENGLAND
England came into being at Noon, 25th December 1066, when William the
Conqueror was crowned in Westminster Abbey. With a Capricorn Sun at midheaven, it would be a slow but sure climb to be a world power. With Aries on the
Ascendant, it would be a war-like and adventurous nation but Moon in Pisces in
the 12th House would give a deceptively reserved persona. This has led England's
enemies to misjudge its aggressive and calculating side once the English are
aroused to anger. Without those qualities it could not, with Cancerian Scotland
as partner, rule a quarter of the world. (Halevi.)

29. History

Britain became an island when the Ice Age ended and melt waters flooded the valley that separated France from what is now England. With the advent of the Age of Aries, migrants crossed the Channel to drive the original inhabitants into Wales and Scotland. Then came the Celts, who fought endless tribal wars until the Romans arrived. According to Ptolemy, the ancient Alexandrian astrologer, the island of Britain was ruled by Aries, the god of war, adventure and innovation.

When Julius Caesar came on a reconnaissance expedition in 55BCE, he found the Britons a formidable enemy. On the August day his ships beached on the Kent coast, Mars was square to Aries while Saturn was in Leo, the sign of imperial Rome. This celestial configuration manifested in a clash between the wild British tribesmen and the disciplined Roman legions. With Saturn as a block on imperial power, Caesar could not, despite beating the Celts back, hold any ground. The time was not right for a full invasion and he withdrew his forces to the Continent. The Celts, however, had seen their island fortress breached.

The next Roman assault came in August 43CE when the Sun was in Leo. This clearly favoured the Romans, while Uranus opposed Aries indicating that the Britons would be afflicted. Indeed, they could not contain the Roman assault this time and so what are now England and Wales, but not Scotland, came under the invaders' rule. Roman rule overlaid the island's zodiacal character in the form of continental culture that connected Britain with the wider world. This situation lasted until 417CE when the legions left the Romano-British on their own because Rome had to defend the empire's frontiers and fight several civil wars. This occurred as Mars and Saturn conjoined and were afflicted in Leo, the zodiacal sign of Italy.

The Roman withdrawal allowed the Anglo-Saxon tribes from Germany to invade Britain and subdue the Celts, driving many from what is now England. These new settlers in turn came under pressure from incoming Vikings who came up the rivers and dominated the coastal areas. These invasions were part of a general Dark Age in western Europe which destroyed civilisation. However, the religious Age of Pisces was well under way and Christian missionaries succeeded in converting much of Britain, so bringing the island under an ecclesiastical form of Roman imperialism. This introduced civilisation to the barbaric English, as they were all now called.

England came into being as a coherent nation when William of Normandy had himself crowned in London at noon on Christmas Day 1066. This gave the kingdom an Aries Ascendant with Sun in Capricorn on the Midheaven and Moon in Pisces in the 12th House. Such a combination gave the country a warlike, strategic mentality with a sentimental mystical streak. The presence of Mercury and Venus in Capricorn added an ability to organise and implement far-reaching plans, while Mars in Aquarius would make the English somewhat eccentric. Jupiter and Saturn in Virgo granted a particular practical thoroughness, especially where their reputation (6th House) was concerned. Uranus in Sagittarius in the 9th House would account for their imperial ambitions while Neptune in Taurus in the 1st House would make them often misjudged as wimpish and deceptive, hence the reputation of 'Perfidious Albion'. The mystical aspect, symbolised by Pluto and Moon in Pisces, would be seen in the distinct lines of witchcraft, Freemasonry and occult orders as well as England's sacred sites and buildings, spiritual music and religious poets such as John Donne and William Blake.

This astrological configuration, the epitome of the English character, imposed its language and culture on Geminian Wales and Taurean Ireland. However, the Welsh played a Mercurial game with the English, who were too Saturnian to understand what was going on, while the Irish Bull stubbornly bellowed in revolts over the centuries. The Scots were a different matter. They were forced into a marriage with England by their own King James VI becoming heir to the English crown and moving to London. As the Cancerian, Watery wife to a domineering Earthy husband, Scotland periodically balked at the Union. Nevertheless she enjoyed the benefits of so rich and powerful a spouse who opened up the world to this clannish community. Such a combination of peoples turned this small collection of offshore islands into the centre of the largest empire ever seen. This was no accident but the destiny of the British.

England, as the core of United Kingdom, is interesting as its rich history records very precisely the effect of astrological transits on its

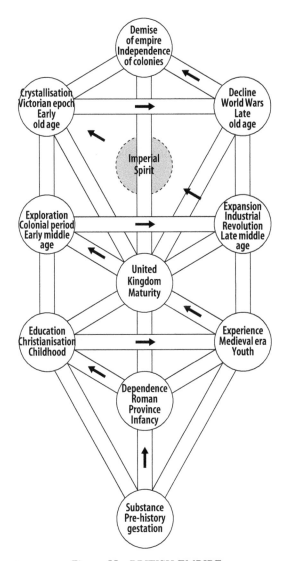

Figure 55—BRITISH EMPIRE
The idea of empire was an invention of Dr John Dee, the occultist and astrologer to Elizabeth I. It began with England's development of American colonies and settling of trade connections throughout the world. Gradually this off-shore island became, with each acquisition, a global power. Britain became the United Kingdom on the First of January 1801; it expanded its territory until Pluto entered Cancer in 1914 and opposed Britain's Capricorn Sun. From then on, it began to decline. Its destiny of industrialisation and modernising the world was done. (Halevi.)

Tree-chart. Take for example the 29-year Saturn cycle. Every time this planet crosses the nation's Ascendant, there is a crisis. An outstanding instance was in 1349, the peak year of the Black Death that killed a quarter of the English population. In the mid 17th century, when Saturn was again in Aries, the great English Civil War between King and Parliament broke out, dividing and ruining the country as bad harvest and famine stalked the land. When the Second World War began in 1939, Saturn had recently conjoined England's Ascendant once more. This conflict exhausted the country and put an end to Britain as a major world power.

The mission of the British Empire produced mixed karma. While it spread the idea of liberal democratic government and a modern infrastructure in its dominions, it exploited the native populations and local resources. The slave trade was a particular blot on a culture that was proud of the Magna Carta which guaranteed certain human rights. Millions had died at British hands and had their land stolen by them and yet, without the Capricornian-Piscean sense of justice and idealistic concern, many ex-colonial countries would have remained at a primitive or barbaric stage of development. Britain brought much of Africa and Asia into the mainstream of modern life. Moreover, English became not only the common language within the empire but the *lingua franca* of the world. It was Britain's destiny to bring together and foster many nations including the United States, its first-born, whose culture is at root Anglo-Saxon, Scandinavian and Celt.

It has been said that the English are the collective reincarnation of a particular soul group. This body of individuals has been moving though history setting up empires that bring different peoples together under a single culture. Such an operation was the ancient Persian empire that was ruled according to just laws, another the regime of the Indian emperor Asoka, who introduced a benign order of government based on Buddhism. Both of these historic entities had a certain character that marked them out as instruments of destiny. The size of a country or population seems to be irrelevant. What is important is the power of the spirit that makes a nation great.

Like people, countries can miss their moment of destiny. Japan, which appears to be ruled by a Scorpio Sun and a Virgo Moon, is a highly disciplined and obedient nation. After centuries of isolation its ruling caste, the Samurai, decided to adapt to the Western methods. They became the militant management class while the rest of the population served the new industrial economy, learning to make, with

Virgoan perfection, the finest of designs and well-made products. This was possible because Japanese society was still essentially feudal. Indeed, everything was done to serve the emperor. To fail was a dishonour for which suicide, a very Scorpionic action, was the correct option among the aristocracy.

When Japan reached an economic and military level equal to the West, which it emulated, it began, like them, to seek to extend its empire. Having gained a foothold on mainland Asia and defeated Russia, it then invaded China in September 1931, just as Mars entered Scorpio. This began a sequence of conquests into all the surrounding countries. The abuse of its power ended abruptly as Mars moved from opposing Scorpio to squaring Virgo on the day the atomic bomb exploded over Hiroshima in August 1945. Japan, which could have led the Far East in peaceful development, failed to carry out its destiny for the general benefit of humanity. Greatness is not about military might.

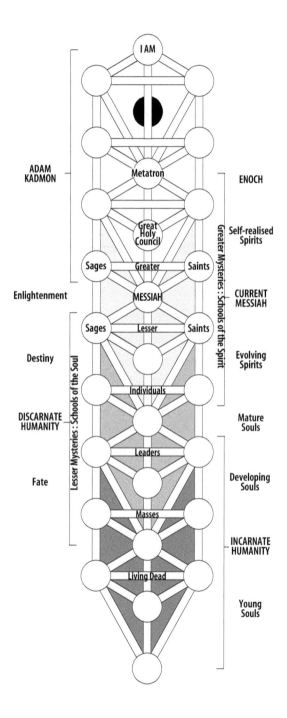

30. Completion

In 1989 when Saturn (repression), Uranus (revolution) and Neptune (idealism) were in Capricorn, the sign of controlling government, the Soviet regimes in eastern Europe collapsed. Russia, ruled by Aquarius, had the opportunity in the 1990s, as Uranus moved through its sign, to put the revolution back on course. In 1917, when Uranus was last in Aquarius, the Bolsheviks had taken over. Stalin, who some say was a reincarnation of Ivan the Terrible, turned the Tsarist empire into the ultimate totalitarian state based upon a ruthless Marxism. Its doctrine of converting the world to Communism was challenged by Hitler's Nazism. The result was that these two monstrous political systems fought each other in a brutal war that probably killed over twenty million people while none of the Western Allies lost more than five hundred thousand dead. This indicates something about the karma of Russia and Germany, both of which imprisoned and executed millions. Japan's war dead were two millions.

The 20th century manifested the negative side of the Aquarian Age with its extreme political and social revolutions. It is clear that, as the third millennium opens, humanity is far from its full potentiality. However, this last century has produced such advances in technology that people can now communicate electronically instantly and travel to the other side of the Earth within twenty-four hours. Perhaps more significant is that any important incident can be known about world-wide, creating the effect of a global village. This is a truly Aquarian phenomenon.

Figure 56 (Left)—SITUATION
This is the state of humanity at present. At the very bottom are those who have abused their birth charts. Next comes the mass of mankind, composed of young souls learning how to live on Earth. Above them are the leaders of every class. Over these are those who are working on their souls. Beyond them come those who have achieved a high degree of development. They serve as the intermediaries between the higher and lower Worlds. The Messiah is the man or woman who currently holds a crucial position between the Divine and incarnate humanity. Finally there is the Great Holy Council, presided over by Metatron/Enoch, the first fully realised human being. (Halevi.)

One of the most remarkable events of the 20th century was the landing on the Moon. Seeing men walking about on its dusty surface united the whole of humanity for a moment as they watched them on television. Just as potent was the image of our planet from space which looked like a living cosmic jewel. For many this was a macrocosmic experience that awakened an awesome sense of the scale of the universe. Never before had humanity perceived their community as a single entity. For several days after the event, which occurred as Mercury conjoined the Sun in Cancer, the masses of mankind felt a distinct bond until local problems began to separate individuals, classes and communities again and people reverted to living under their Moons and no longer under their Suns.

Fortunately the great wave of interest in spirituality, especially in the West and due to Neptune being in Scorpio and Pluto in Virgo, was moving hundreds of thousands of people to take up meditation or seek out higher knowledge. More books were published on esoteric matters than there had ever been and groups studying and practising various spiritual disciplines flourished. This is the Neptune in Scorpio factor while Pluto in Virgo stimulated many to take up yoga, enter some psychological therapy or study alternative medicine.

This worldwide phenomenon was a sign that humanity is beginning to mature and operate as a unit again, after hundreds of thousands of years of separation since it first emerged from Africa. Such unifying organisations as the United Nations, the European Union and many other collective cultural, commercial and political associations indicated that the world was becoming smaller and more safe. The problems of pollution, famine and war were recognised; so too was the issue of overpopulation, although it appeared that the planet had taken this into account by reducing the male sperm count.

The implication of these events is that the plan of Evolution is proceeding despite human aggression and greed. The only possibility of stopping humanity's development would be an atomic war which even an insane tyrant would hardly contemplate for fear of retaliation. The Age of Aquarius and its impulse of social change is moving nations away from dictatorship towards democracy. While this may be an imperfect political system, it does allow the individual to participate in government and the development of millions as responsible citizens.

All this adds to the stimulation of individuation and the raising of the general level of consciousness. This in turn accelerates the

Figure 57—ASTROLOGICAL ADAM KADMON
This is a medieval version of the celestial image of God. It contains, like Adam
Kadmon, every type of person who, over many lives, lives out the whole zodiac.
This cycle is part of the process of descent and ascent which will be complete
when all have experienced what each Sign can illuminate. When this is done,
then the End of Time will come as we all return to Adam Kadmon who is a SELF
portrait of the Absolute. Then God will behold God and I AM will become One
before disappearing into NO-THING-Ness again.

transformation of animal people into a more humane mode and moves the young souls of the vegetable masses on a grade. Meantime those who have attained a degree of self-awareness will increase in number while those who have reached the level where they have learnt their lessons can execute their missions to help humanity onwards.

Figure 56 sets out the situation of the four journeys. At the first level are those young souls who are learning about life and death on Earth. They oscillate in the cycle of reincarnation between the two lower Worlds. The second stage is of those gradually ascending through psychological development by working on their karma and, if they happen to be kabbalistic astrologers, their Tree-charts or fate. The third journey is for those people of destiny who decide to descend to aid evolving individuals, through schools of the soul or communities, by being either open or hidden leaders and teachers.

The fourth and final journey is for those great individuals who have completed all their missions and can return, karma-free, to the upper region of the spiritual World after receiving enlightenment. They may come down to Earth by choice, from time to time, to start a new religion or period in history. The people who belong to this class are those who have been the Messiah, Buddha or Axis of the Age.

At the end of this vast and long process, known as the Resurrection in several esoteric traditions, humanity would have reached a point when all but the most obstinate or perverse would have met and reunited with their soul mate, rejoined their original spiritual group and begun to turn towards the Divine from whence they came. This final journey for all will occur when each person finds their own place in the being of Adam Kadmon.

Upon this happening, each human cell of the Divine body will be self-realised to the full and the primordial image of God will say, so tradition has it, I AM THAT I AM. Then God will behold God in this reflection of all Existence.

If this book on kabbalistic astrology has helped to deepen your understanding of the anatomy of fate, destiny and purpose in the universe, then I shall have succeeded in part of my mission.

Z'ev ben Shimon Halevi
December 1999, London

Glossary of Terms

Affliction	Tense geometrical angle between celestial bodies.
Air signs	Gemini, Libra, Aquarius.
Ascendant	Zodiacal degree on the Eastern horizon.
Asiyyah	Elemental and Natural World.
Aspect	Angular relationship between celestial bodies.
Ayin	No-thing-ness of the Absolute.
Azilut	Divine World of Emanation.
Benefics	Friendly planets: Jupiter and Venus.
Beriah	World of Creation, spirit, ideas, heaven and archangels.
Binah	Sefirah of Understanding, reason and Saturn.
Cardinal signs	Dynamic signs: Aries, Cancer, Libra and Capricorn.
Conjunction	Celestial bodies in close proximity by zodiacal degree.
Daat	Non-sefirah of mystical knowledge and Pluto.
Descendant	Diametric opposite of Ascendant, symbolising the Western horizon.
Dragon's Head,	
Dragon's Tail	Alternative names for North and South Lunar Nodes.
Earth signs	Taurus, Virgo and Capricorn.
Elements	Classification of signs as Air, Earth, Fire or Water.
En Sof	Infinite Endless All of Absolute.
Equinox	Point in March and September at which the Sun crosses the Equator.
Fire signs	Aries, Leo and Sagittarius.
Fixed signs	Taurus, Leo, Scorpio and Aquarius.
Gevurah	Sefirah of Judgement, emotional control and Mars.
Great Year	A complete cycle of the twelve Ages of Aries, Pisces, Aquarius etc, lasting around 2,000-2,500 years each.
Hesed	Sefirah of Mercy, emotional expansion and Jupiter.
Hod	Sefirah of Reverberation, communication and Mercury.

Hokhmah	Sefirah of Wisdom, revelation and Uranus.
Houses	Twelvefold division of the horoscope concerned with manifestation in the world.
Individuation	Development of selfhood.
Inferior planets	Planets with orbits between Earth and the Sun: Mercury and Venus.
Keter	Sefirah of Crown, the Divine and Neptune.
Malefics	Unfriendly planets: Mars and Saturn.
Malkhut	Sefirah of Kingdom, four elements and Earth. Ascendant.
Mutable signs	Changeable and volatile signs: Gemini, Virgo, Sagittarius and Pisces.
Natal chart	Horoscope made of the celestial situation at birth.
Nezah	Sefirah of Repetition, instinct and Venus.
(Lunar) Nodes	Areas of ease and difficulty in horoscope.
Opposition	Strong aspect between celestial bodies diametrically opposed to each other.
Precession	Apparent backward motion of the equinoxes around the zodiac over a Great Year.
Progression	Method of advancing the horoscope into the future, eg. one degree represents one year.
Quadruplicities	Classification of signs according to four elements in Cardinal, Fixed and Mutable modes.
Retrograde	The apparent backward motion of celestial bodies, indicating a restraining influence.
Ruling planet	The celestial body that rules a particular sign, eg. Sun and Leo.
Sefirah, Sefirot	Divine principle/principles of Tree of Life.
Sefirotic Tree	Diagram of Tree of Life.
Self	The essence of an individual, the Solar and Tiferet position in the Tree of Psyche.
Sextile	Mild, favourable aspect between celestial bodies.
Solstice	Point in June/December where the Sun is furthest North/South of the Equator.
Square	A difficult aspect between celestial bodies.
Superior planets	Planets with orbits further from the Sun than that of Earth: Mars, Jupiter, Saturn, Uranus, Neptune and Pluto.
Tiferet	Sefirah of Beauty, central principle, self and Sun.
Transit	Actual movement of celestial bodies over or through crucial areas of horoscope.

Tree of Life	Sefirotic diagram.
Trine	Easy and very favourable aspect between celestial bodies.
Triplicities	Classification of signs that share the same element.
Water signs	Cancer, Scorpio and Pisces.
Yesod	Sefirah of Foundation, ego and Moon.
Yezirah	World of Formation, angels, Paradise and psyche.
Zodiac	A band of twelve divisions of the sky along which the celestial bodies move, as seen from the Earth.

Lightning Source UK Ltd.
Milton Keynes UK
UKHW020601190619
344635UK00003B/192/P